START-UP to
SCALE-UP:

BUYING A BUSINESS

David Johnson and Jerry Corvino

ISBN: 1-4392-1222-8
ISBN-13: 9781439212226

Table of Contents

Chapter 3-Selling Yourself to Sellers

Chapter 4-Building Your Advisory Team

Chapter 5-Finding a Business

Chapter 6-A Word About the Selling Prospectus

Chapter 7-Assessing the Business Financials

Chapter 8-Assessing the Non-Financial Issues

8.1 The Seller

8.2 The Company

8.3 Employees

8.4 Customers

8.5 Equipment

8.6 Suppliers

8.7 General Industry Conditions

8.8 Competition

8.9 Technology

8.10 Regulatory Issues

Chapter 9-Deal Structure Is Everything

9.1 Asset Sales and Stock Sales

9.2 Seller Financing

9.3 Allocation of Purchase Price

9.4 Consulting and Employer Agreements

Chapter 10-Financing the Deal

10.1 Estimating the Financial Need

10.2 Sources of Funding

10.3 Getting the Funds

Chapter 11-The Right Price

11.1 What Is the Right Price?

11.2 Net Cash Flow

11.3 Principal and Interest Coverage

11.4 Discounted Cash Flow

11.5 What the Market Will Bear

Chapter 1

Should You Buy a Small Business?

In this chapter, we will:
* Present an overview of small business statistics in the United States (U.S.)
* Discuss the personal attributes necessary for success
* Discuss personal financial requirements
* Review personal goals

1.1   SMALL BUSINESS FACTS

The federal government of the U.S. established the Small Business Administration (SBA) as an independent agency in 1953. The mission of the U.S. SBA is to "maintain and strengthen the economy of the nation by aiding, counseling, assisting, and protecting the interests of small businesses and by preserving free competitive enterprise in the U.S." The SBA also helps families and businesses recover from national disasters.

The website of the SBA (http://www.sba.gov) is an excellent resource for information on small businesses. The SBA defines a "small business," for the purpose of research, as an independent business having fewer than 500 employees.

The following statistics are available on the SBA website (http://www.sba.gov/advo/news.html)

- ❖ In 2005, the Office of Advocacy, U.S. SBA, estimated there were 25.8 million businesses in the U.S.
- ❖ Of those 25.8 million businesses, 99.9 percent were classified as small businesses.
- ❖ Estimates for opening new firms and closure of existing small businesses showed similar trends. Nearly 10 percent of the total businesses in 2005 were either new firms or closures. There were an estimated 671,800 new firms and 544,800 closures.
- ❖ The U.S. Bureau of the Census estimates that 60–80 percent of all net jobs are created by small businesses over the past decade.
- ❖ In 2000-2001 (according to the most recent data), small businesses created all of the net new jobs in the U.S.
- ❖ Small businesses represent 99.7 percent of all employers.
- ❖ Small businesses employ 50 percent of all private sector employees.
- ❖ Small businesses pay 44.3 percent of the total U.S. private payroll.
- ❖ Two-thirds of new employer firms survive at least two years, and about half survive at least four years. Owners of about one-third of the firms that closed said their firm was successful at closure.
- ❖ Six percent of small businesses fail each year if we eliminate the owner-identified "successful" businesses from the closures.

A business is not guaranteed to be a success, regardless of your intelligence or effort. You improve your chances of success by buying an established, successful business rather than starting a business from scratch. After all, the previous owner has created a product or provided a service, attracted customers, hired employees, and made money. You will confirm all of that in the process of selecting and buying a business through a process of due diligence.

1.1   IT IS ALL ABOUT YOU

What does it take to be successful?

Businesses may have active owners or absentee owners. We see many more active ownership businesses come up for sale because the owner is retiring, has died, or is liquidating the business for some other reason (e.g., divorce or health). Successful small businesses with absentee ownership are not often put up for sale. The current owner would probably keep the business if the business could be successful with him or her as an absentee owner. What is the ownership of your target business?

Active owner participation is more likely to lead your business to success. You can expect to spend significant time taking over and running the business. We recommend that you learn all aspects of the business in detail, even if the infrastructure and staff for successful operation are in place. Your period of success with the business, after the settling-in period of up to one year, will probably be about the same as the current owner, if you do not change business objectives (e.g., high growth versus steady state). While we are at it, here is another truth—businesses rarely run themselves. (We will discuss more of these truths in later chapters.) You need to lead the business to success. How much time are you willing to spend actively managing or leading the business?

Circumstances change. The market conditions that create a successful business today may not exist in a year or two. Construction-related businesses were doing extremely well in Nevada (Las Vegas), Arizona, and southern California two years ago, but today they are enduring a severe and lengthy downturn. Are you ready to invest your energy and creativity to guarantee continued business success in the face of difficult conditions?

Are you willing to put in the time and energy to learn the skills you need to be successful? For instance, you may need to invest in additional training for a license, or general business training in issues relating to human resource management or accounting.

This would also be a good time to consider how owning this business will impact your ability to travel or take a vacation. How often did the current owners take a break? Did the business run well when they were not around? What will happen to the business if you are gone for a few months on an around-the-world cruise? Who will be minding the store?

An entrepreneur can be defined as a person who organizes and manages a business undertaking, assuming the risk for the sake of the profit. How do you feel about risk? In later chapters, we will lay out a process to minimize the risk in buying a business, but the risk will never be zero. You could lose your entire investment—and even more, including your house! Pulling a statistic from the previous chapter, 6 percent of small businesses fail every year. Can you handle the risk?

It is all about you. Your time, energy, tolerance for risk, and creativity can make a successful business. Do not buy a business if you are unwilling or unable to invest the time as well as the money.

1.2 FINANCIAL CONSIDERATIONS

Cash is required to buy a business. We favor a leveraged purchase financed by the seller (preferable), a private banking arrangement, or the Small Business Administration (SBA). You will need money for a down payment and working capital (we will discuss more on working capital in Chapter 2). We prefer to provide about 30 percent of the purchase price plus the working capital. For example, if the business is for sale for $2 million and requires $200,000 in working capital, we recommend a $660,000 investment and a loan of $1,540,000. As a very rough rule of thumb, assume you should have at least $330,000 as cash in hand for every $1 million in purchase price. Your risk will increase significantly if you invest less.

You need to decide how much you are willing to invest from your savings or other investments. Your bank or other lending institutions will decide your credit worthiness, and they may be willing to loan you more than you are comfortable borrowing. The caveat here is this: you will likely be personally guaranteeing the loan. The business does not guarantee the loan. The amount you are willing to invest will determine the size and profitability of the business you can buy.

Small businesses often get into trouble because they are undercapitalized. Buyers invest all the liquid assets they have in buying the business, and then they need cash to increase inventory or purchase equipment. Are you able and willing to invest more money to make the business grow? We would, of course, prefer that the business generate enough cash after tax payments to handle these investments. What will you do if the cash isn't available for operating the business?

1.3 PERSONAL GOALS

People typically buy a business for one of three reasons:

1. To make a living. People get tired of working for someone else and believe they have what it takes to start or buy their own business. They intend to live on the income from the business, so failure is not an option. They understand a significant effort is required and plan to do whatever it takes to be successful.

2. To have some fun. They have always been interested in expensive hobbies like sports cars, horses, travel, or some other pursuit. They decide to own a business in a related area to offset the cost of that activity. They understand the business needs to make some money, or the IRS will deem it a hobby and not a business (talk to your accountant for more information). But they are not looking to work eighty hours per week to build a large, highly profitable business.

3. To have some fun and make some money. This is often the case with semi-retired corporate executives. They have "enough" money to live on, but are bored and need something productive to do. Or they want to supplement their retirement income. The cost of living keep going up and they may find it difficult to enhance, or even maintain, their lifestyle. Their investments are not generating much return, and they decide that their own business would have a better return on the invested cash. They are willing to work to guarantee the return on the investment (ROI), but don't want to work eleven hours per day, seven days a week either.

You will often hear a business described as a "lifestyle" business. One business broker we know defined a lifestyle business as "any business where you could bring your dog to work." Lifestyle does not necessarily mean small or home-based. We visited a significant (over U.S. $3 million in revenue) HVAC company with an office staff of eight people and found five small dogs that had the run of the office. Is that a lifestyle business?

It is very important to pick a goal. We suggest that you write it down. Look at it carefully. Revise it as many times as you wish until you are satisfied with your goal. A goal is not made in one day, or even seven days for that matter. Test any business you might buy against your goal. Will you have fun with the business? How much effort are you looking at to ensure success? Will the business generate enough money for you to live happily?

Talk over the goal with your spouse, partner, or significant other. We almost always see a couple actively involved in successful small businesses we review as potential purchases. They share the workload and reduce business expense by not having an additional employee.

1.4   FINAL THOUGHTS

Do not even start looking for a business to buy until you understand your financial situation and your goals. Unfortunately, people sometimes fall in love with a particular business before ensuring it fits with their goals and financial situation. They get into the process of selection without due diligence, and they like the owner or love the perceived profit. Subsequently, they find out that they need to work seven days a week and ten hours a day to have a reasonably successful business.

They might have realized this before buying the business if they had followed the due diligence.

It is difficult to not get caught up in the thrill of the hunt. The process we outline will identify a business that is right for you, not just a business that might be financially successful. If you buy a business that is financially successful but keeps you from enjoying life, what have you gained?

Chapter 2
Narrowing Your Search

In this chapter, we will:

* Build off the goals we set for buying a business in Chapter 1
* Utilize the five filter approach to zero in on the right business to buy

The U.S. is a free and competitive market, with plenty of people buying and selling businesses. A large online business listing service currently has over 1,000 businesses listed for sale in California alone! It could take months or even years to review each of these opportunities. The best place to start would be with your clear and specific goals regarding your business. How do you zero in on that once-in-a-lifetime opportunity that is made just for you?

We have a systematic process, using a checklist of five filters, to narrow down the search and identify the right business. The Five Filter Approach (FFA), as we call it, is a common-sense approach that builds off your personal business goals.

The Five Filter Approach to Identify the Right Business to Buy
❖ Location ❖ Industry ❖ Size ❖ Work/Life ❖ Affordability

2.1 LOCATION

A good location is the heart of any business. The right location will go a long way in keeping your business in good health.

Home is where the heart lies, and many people prefer buying a business closer to home. Besides, there are several advantages to owning a business that is closer to one's home.

For one, you are familiar with the economy. You have lived in the area and are aware of the factors that drive the local economy. You know what works well and what does not work as well in the area. For example, many small manufacturing companies in California find the cost of doing business (e.g., labor, workers' compensation insurance, etc.) too high to compete with out-of-state companies. If you have your heart set on buying a widget manufacturer (a commodity product), you may want to consider a business-friendly state (Arizona or Nevada, rather than California). You may want to consider the number of new housing developments in the area if you are interested in a construction-related business (electrical, HVAC, roofing, etc.). Are housing prices and the local population increasing or stagnant? Have a lot of companies gone out of business or moved out of the area? Research may answer these questions, but cannot replace the experience gained from living with the local situation.

The yellow pages provide an easy-to-use, free list of businesses organized by industry that might be for sale at the right price. You can "cold call" the businesses in your area. You do not have to spend much time and resources researching these businesses, since you live in the area. You may already be familiar with some of them! You may have seen a business that fits with your personal business goals. It never hurts to ask, even if the business is not currently listed for sale. You never know, the current owners may be willing to sell the business. If not, they may keep you in mind if they consider selling at a later date.

There may be circumstances such that you want to make a clean break and start a new chapter of your life. You may want to buy a business in a new area and relocate to some place you have never lived before. At times like these, the Internet comes in handy. The World Wide Web has made it easy to buy a business anywhere! The Internet provides plenty of information about local economies, population trends, climate, business regulations, etc. It may not be as good as living in the area, but there is plenty of information to help you make informed decisions. We will discuss more about finding a business in Chapter 5.

You can choose to be a remote owner of your business. This is often the case when the business is located elsewhere and can run itself without your direct on-site involvement. It is a happy situation where you get the best of both worlds. You get to stay where you live now, plus own a business that runs itself. If you think this sounds too utopian—it is. These options are not as picture-perfect as they look. You have to always be on top of the local business climate, the number of competitors, regulatory issues, and so on to successfully manage a business through remote ownership. As we mentioned earlier, successful businesses that are represented as remote ownership opportunities are not often put up for sale. And our take on this is—proceed cautiously if you see a remote-owned business for sale (more on this in Chapter 6).

One final note on location: if you decide to buy a business in another area and you plan to be a resident owner, include the cost of relocation in your financial planning. Some of you may have moved earlier as part of a corporate relocation, so you would appreciate that there is a significant cost associated with such a move. As an owner of your own business, you are paying the full cost of the relocation, even if the cost is being reimbursed by the new business. In essence, you are reimbursing yourself. Owners of a business often fall into the trap of believing that relocation (or any other expense) reimbursement is a non-expense or is coming from someplace else. It all adds up to the bottom line and is always your money!

2.2 INDUSTRY

You understood your personal business goals (the why) from Chapter 1 and decided the likely business location (the where) in the previous section.

In this section, we will decide the "what." We will now:

- Present the "big" question
- Review a simple industry segmentation approach
- Identify particular issues with some industries

1. The big question: Something old or something new? In other words, are you looking for a business that you are familiar with?

Most people decide to buy a business in an industry they already know. Electricians buy electrical contractors. Truck drivers buy trucking companies. The advantage is obvious: you already know a lot about the business. You have been working in that area for years or decades. You believe you can do it better and believe you have what it takes to be the boss. You understand the regulatory requirements and may already have the required licenses or experience needed to get the license. For example, to qualify for an electrical contractor's license (L11) in Arizona, you need four years of related experience.

Now, consider a situation where you want to buy a business that you are not familiar with. Is there a business you have been interested in trying out, but have put off because you have no practical experience? For instance, do you work on your own cars and think it would be great to own an auto repair business? The more knowledge you have (even as an amateur), the easier it will be to take over and successfully run the business. It is always preferable to know the business going in, especially if the business meets your other goals.

Running the business and working for the business present totally different challenges. As a worker, you could just focus on your work and hope the rest would take care of itself. As the owner, you have to worry about hiring and firing, managing cash flow, litigation, regulation, customer service, etc.— the whole nine yards. You will obviously have an advantage in matters related to your specific areas of expertise; for instance, wiring a house. However, you may not currently have all the skills to run the business. You may have to learn these new skills, or hire someone who has the necessary skill sets. If you hire someone, you have to pay them. In other words, you need to balance between investing in training yourself and hiring a new person.

2. Segment the industry: Some buyers say, "We are here to make money. We do not care what industry we get into as long as the greenbacks keep rolling in." Unfortunately, it does not always work that way in the real world. You cannot invest wisely in an industry you do not care about or do not understand. You will not get good returns if you cannot invest wisely.

How do you find the industry that interests you? First, we need to find a way to focus our search efforts on a reasonable number of industry segments and companies.

There are many ways to segment industries. The North American Industry Classification Systems (NAICS) is maintained by the United States, Canada, and Mexico. The NAICS replaces the old United States Standard Industrial Classification (SIC) codes. (For more information see http://www.census.gov/epcd/www/naics.html.) NAICS is overly detailed for our purposes. There are 1,180 six-digit NAICS codes alone! NAICS codes are useful in researching a specific industry or business. However, you could use this list to give you some ideas about what to look for.

What we really need is a simpler classification system that will help us find the business we want faster. We find the following categories sufficient to narrow our search:

- ❖ Activity: product (manufacturing) or service
- ❖ Customers: business to business or business to consumer
- ❖ Office: home-based or office

Service sector businesses are the fastest-growing part of the U.S. economy. Product businesses can be vulnerable to offshore competition (think China). In either case, you need a business with a barrier to entry high enough that a new entrant cannot easily drive you out of business. Some industries, especially those dealing with commodity products or services, are extremely fragmented (e.g., there are more than fifty vending machine operators in Las Vegas). Achieving sustainable profitability in a commodity product or service business is not easy. Think through each of these issues and eliminate potential business opportunities after identifying issues that are most important to your business.

3. Identify issues: Are you ready to deal directly with the public? You have probably been in a retail outlet, restaurant, or other consumer-oriented establishment and seen how difficult a business it can be. Do not choose a customer-oriented business if you are not comfortable in a sales-driven environment, dealing with the public on a regular basis.

Working from home sounds like a great idea (no commute), but requires a great deal of discipline and some personal as well as physical space. There may be more distractions at home, unless you live alone. Do you have a comfortable home office where you wouldn't mind spending four to ten hours daily? Will customers, suppliers, employees, and so forth come to the "office," which also doubles as your home? Are you comfortable with bringing work home? Is your family comfortable with your bringing work home?

2.3   SIZE

There are three major considerations, excluding cost, with respect to the size of the business you will be buying:

- Number of employees
- Number of locations
- Complexity

The number and type of employees has a significant impact on managing the business. For example, restaurants typically have a large number of full- and part-time employees (cooks, servers, etc.) to cover a seven-day-per-week schedule. Employee turnover can be a significant issue in these businesses. You have to be comfortable with recruiting and hiring people if you plan to be in a business that has a high turnover of personnel. An example from the American Trucking Association, May 2005, is indicative of the demands that may be placed on your skills: "Of the 3.4 million truck drivers on the road, 1.3 million are long-haul truckers, which is the driver segment most severely impacted by the shortage. Although the current driver shortage is set at 20,000 drivers, it seems larger to the industry because of a high degree of driver 'churning,' or moving from carrier to carrier. Large truckload carriers reported an average annual employee turnover of 121% last year."

Every industry has specific management issues that need to be addressed. Do your homework. Google may be your best friend by the time this is finished. Make sure you understand the issues in advance and are willing to deal with them.

Even small businesses can have multiple locations that require your presence. How many locations are you willing to deal with, and how much time are you willing to spend moving from location to location? We have looked at a construction-related business with annual revenue that was less than $3 million.

This business had a factory in Tijuana and a shop in San Diego County. Whoever buys this business has to travel to Tijuana, crossing the border every week. We also looked at another business with operations at least two and a half hours apart (if one was lucky enough not to get caught in traffic). Small does not necessarily mean consolidated.

Here's another thought to chew on. If you've never owned a business before, your life is about to get a lot more complicated. You may be dealing with many issues for the first time:

❖ Human resources (hiring, firing)
❖ Payroll law
❖ Workers' compensation
❖ Business insurance
❖ Licensing
❖ Accounting and bookkeeping
❖ Leasing
❖ Foreign law and import-export regulations
❖ Contracting

With all these issues, the size of the business matters. The bigger the business, the larger the scale of issues you need to grapple with. It is better to have a good idea of what you are comfortable dealing with before starting the search.

2.4   WORK/LIFE CHOICES

How hard do you want to work? Are you (or your spouse) looking for a business to "get you out of the house?" Will the business be your primary source of income? Are you willing to work as hard as necessary, to give it your all?

Do you want to work with your spouse, significant other, or children? A family-owned business has its advantages, especially with respect to workforce. However, you have to be cautious about the potential for family dynamics to affect the business. A number of businesses are currently for sale specifically because the family members want nothing to do with the business—or each other—anymore.

While we do not have any quick-fix solutions to offer, we want to highlight the fact that there are many choices that you and your family need to consider before you buy a specific business.

2.5 AFFORDABILITY

You are about to make the biggest single purchase of your life. What follows is a very simple approach to the "first cut" on what you can afford, based on your current liquid assets. The process described below will help you eliminate businesses you cannot afford, or that do not meet your income requirements. This approach yields a rough idea of affordability, without doing a huge amount of financial analysis. A simple spreadsheet or paper and pencil table will suffice for this analysis.

The obligatory disclaimer: we are not financial planners, lawyers, or accountants. We will provide you with a simple, easy to use set of criteria for a "first cut" on the available businesses that meet the other criteria described above. You should contact your financial planner or accountant before proceeding with any transaction.

We make the following assumptions for the purposes of this discussion:

❖ You will finance or leverage the business. Some part of the purchase price will come from a lending institution, with or without the Small Business Administration. We also assume that you will use your existing funds to put 30 percent of the purchase price into the transaction. (We will discuss more on financing in Chapter 10.)

❖ Post sale, you will provide working capital for the daily operations of the business. Working capital, for the purpose of this discussion, is the cash necessary to pay the startup expenses (e.g., licenses, insurance, utility deposits, etc.) and pay the bills, until the cash from operating the business starts rolling in. The need for working capital varies from business to business. We typically assume 5–10 percent of the annual revenues (not the purchase price) will be sufficient. (Working capital requirements are covered in more detail in Chapter 10.)

❖ There is no real estate involved in the affordability analysis. In fact, many small businesses are sold with an option for purchasing real estate. The separate, but related, real estate transaction should be evaluated on its merits, and is beyond the scope of this discussion.

❖ Inventory, supplies, fixtures, furniture, and equipment (FF&E) are included in the price.

❖ You know how much money you need or want as an income out of the business.

❖ The selling prospectus provides the owner's or adjusted cash flow. Owner's cash flow is the sum of the net profit of the company, the owner's salary and fringes, any legitimate onetime expenses, and all amortization, depreciation, and interest payments. It is very important to fully understand owner's cash flow (we will discuss it further in Chapter 6).

❖ Principal and interest coverage (P&I ratio) is the ratio of the buyer's adjusted cash flow to the annual principal and interest payments for financing the business purchase. We use this as a measure of risk. You need some headroom to allow for the natural cycles and seasonal variations in business. You need more coverage if you do not want to invest more money after you buy the business, if the business is seasonal or cyclic in nature. The following table lists some rules of thumb that will help you evaluate the measurement.

Ratio	Interpretation
<1.0	The business will not support itself.
1.0 to 1.6	Marginal business. A downturn in revenues or increase in costs could result in more cash being required to stay in business. Buyer's compensation at some risk.
1.6 to 2.0	Good business. Should be able to cover expenses except in extreme downturn. Buyer's compensation should be secure.
>=2.0	Great business. Low risk of additional cash requirements.

❖ Buyer's adjusted cash flow (BCF) is the owner's adjusted cash flow minus the new principal and interest payments and any new expenses (e.g., leasing the property back from the seller rather than buying it). In capital-intensive businesses (e.g., long-haul trucking company), this amount would be further reduced by the estimated annual capital requirement for equipment. Buyer's adjusted cash flow is the cash available for your salary and fringes. How much money do you need (or want) to make from this business?

Let's run through some examples. These companies represent real companies for sale at the time of writing this book. The descriptions have been modified to protect the privacy and confidentiality of the parties involved.

2.5.1   EXAMPLE 1-STONE BUSINESS

The business provides and installs stone products primarily in new housing developments. The business is listed for sale at $2 million. The annual revenue is $2.5 million, and the owner's cash flow is $500,000. We will use 10 percent of the gross sales as the working capital requirement, since the startup expenses are low and the housing developers tend to pay in thirty to sixty days. The current business premises will be leased at the same annual cost. A five-year loan with a principal amount of $1,400,000 at 7 percent will be required to finance the purchase. The annual P&I payment is $341,447.

1.   How much cash do you need as down payment to buy this business?
     Cash: (.3 x $2,000,000) + (.1 x 2,500,000) = $850,000

2.   What is the principal and interest coverage?
     P&I Ratio: $500,000 / $341,447 = 1.5

3.   What is the buyer's cash flow (BCF)?
     BCF = $500,000 - $341,447 = $158,553

We would not pursue this business, since the buyer's cash flow and the principal and interest coverage are too low for comfort.

2.5.2   EXAMPLE 2-DOCUMENT MANAGEMENT

The business provides document management services to medical facilities. The business is listed for sale at $2,500,000. The annual revenue is $4,600,000, and the owner's cash flow is $1,000,000. We will use 10 percent of the gross sales for the working capital requirement, as the startup expenses are low and the customers tend to pay in thirty to sixty days. The current business premises will be leased at the same annual cost. A five-year loan with a principal of $2,072,000 at 7.5 percent will be required to finance the purchase. The annual P&I payment is $512,125.

1. How much cash do you need as down payment to buy this business?
   Cash: (.3 x $2,500,000) + (.1 x $4,600,000) = $1,200,000
2. What is the principal and interest coverage?
   P&I Ratio: $1,000,000 / $512,125 = 1.95
3. What is the buyer's cash flow (BCF)?
   BCF = $1,000,000 - $512,125 = $487,875

This business is worth pursuing, since the buyer's cash flow and the principal and interest coverage are good.

2.6   SUMMARY

In this chapter, we identified a number of selection criteria or filters to identify the businesses worth pursuing from among the thousands of businesses up for sale. We recommend understanding the selection criteria before actually searching for a business (see Chapter 5), for two reasons. First, you may decide you do not want to buy a business. Second, you do not want to waste significant time and effort investigating or even negotiating to buy a business that does not generate enough cash or is too complex for you to own.

Chapter 3
Selling Yourself to Sellers

In this chapter, we will cover:
* Why you need to sell yourself
* What sellers and business brokers look for
* How to prepare your Buyer Information Package
* How to convince sellers that you are the one
* A sample buyer page
* A sample Buyer Information Package

3.1   WHY DO YOU HAVE TO SELL YOURSELF?

You're the one writing the big check, right? The seller must want to sell; otherwise, he would not have the business on the market. Why should you worry about selling yourself?

Here's the deal. You are unlikely to get the business you want without doing a fair bit of selling yourself. If you are working through business brokers, you may not even get to meet the seller unless the broker is convinced of your credentials. You need to convince people that you are serious about buying a business before they part with information about businesses that might fit the bill.

Why? Because there are many potential buyers for every good business that is up for sale. Buying a business is almost like buying a desirable house in a hot market. But unlike that desirable house in the hot market, which costs money to own and maintain, a business keeps generating cash for the owner (at least the good ones do). That means a seller is making money while waiting to sell the business. He can afford to wait, or even take the business off the market and try again later. Of course, there are the inevitable distress sales, but these are rarely the types of good businesses that you will want to snap up quickly.

Besides, any seller goodwill that you generate will come into play when the deal is done and the business is yours. A strong recommendation from the seller to customers, employees, and suppliers can be invaluable in getting off to a good start. Creating goodwill with sellers and their business brokers is the key to your success in buying and taking over the right business. And it is not tough. All it takes is some careful preparation from your side.

3.2   WHAT ARE SELLERS LOOKING FOR?

1. Financial qualifications

Sellers are looking for a financial gain when they put their business on the market. They will be keenly interested in your ability to deliver the price that has been agreed upon. Unfortunately, there are large numbers of potential buyers who cannot deliver on this front. All too often, people are "window shopping" for businesses without the ability to actually close the deal. Others want to close the deal but are unable to get adequate financing. We spoke to one broker in the Southeast who had recently put a construction-related business on the market. He confided that he had received thirty expressions of interest in the two months the business had been on the market. Only one of those offers had any financial qualification. Be ready to prove your financial qualifications (or better still, over-qualification) to buy the business. This will help you get a jump start over the masses of unqualified buyers. You will at least have a seat at the table to talk with a seller who is willing to hear your pitch.

2. The right fit

Sellers usually have a complicated relationship with their business, almost similar to a parent-child relationship. Sellers will have a pride of ownership; after all, the seller has built the business up to where it attracts your attention today. The seller may also be concerned about the well-being of employees that will be transferred along with the business. Businesses often bear the name of the owner, or are easily recognized by the community as associated with the owner. For these reasons and others, sellers usually have a strong desire to see the business go to "the right buyer." This desire is also fueled by any financial arrangements that tie the owner's ultimate payout to the health of the business, such as consulting contracts, owner carry-back notes, or earn-outs. You want your child to move with the right crowd. Most sellers want to know that you will be successful with their business.

3. Speed

For most sellers, having their business on the market is an unpleasant experience. It means more work for the seller. Also, there is a real risk that the process could hurt the business. The risk comes in many forms, but the most common is that the customers, employees, or suppliers of the business learn of the impending sale and react in a way that is detrimental to the health of the business. One seller of a $10 million business sold last year learned this the hard way. Two key employees of the company learned about the pending transaction and quit the next day. The suppliers to the company quickly learned of the deal from the former employees. The suppliers promptly put the company on Cash on Delivery (COD) terms, destroying years of goodwill built by the owner to get ninety-day payment terms. The COD terms significantly increased the amount of working capital required to run the business, rendering it unattractive to buy.

Buyers and sellers can work together to minimize the risk. However, the potential for risk is there until the deal is closed. The owner carries the entire burden of risk during this period. The faster a seller can go from listing a business to closing the deal, the lesser the risk they will be exposed to. Sellers prefer dealing with someone who will move quickly through the process and not dither around less important issues. A buyer who is not financially qualified can spend months trying to access funds. A buyer who is financially qualified can move faster through the process without being held up.

4. Trust

Trust is a two-way street. Without it, the deal simply won't happen for either party. Sellers need to know that they can trust a buyer through the due diligence process when they are handing over their most confidential business information. They also need to trust that you will move as quickly as possible, and will deliver on promises made during the course of the agreement, be it an agreed upon closing date, treatment of particular employees after the deal closes, or just keeping quiet about the upcoming deal. Everything of importance to both parties should be covered in the signed purchase agreement. But without trust, the contract often amounts to little more than the value of the paper.

3.3   WHAT ARE BROKERS LOOKING FOR?

We will discuss brokers at length in Chapter 5. For the purpose of this discussion, it is useful to note two major facts about business brokers. First, brokers rely on their good reputation (and a lot of marketing) to bring them a steady stream of sellers willing to engage their services. Second, brokers are paid a commission when a transaction is completed.

1. Filtering

One of a broker's major functions is to filter the buyers before presenting them to the seller. Brokers who bring potential buyers who are not financially qualified or who are just window shopping will find their reputation eroding. When you introduce yourself to a broker, they will assess whether you meet the requirements of the seller.

2. Commission-based earnings

Brokers get paid when the deal is closed. As discussed in the previous section, any potential buyer who is unlikely to close a deal is of very little interest to a broker. Therefore, the broker is very motivated to determine, in the shortest amount of time possible, if a buyer is a real prospect or not. As they are not paid by the hour to deal with the legions of potential buyers that call in to their offices, they will not invest too much time working with you until they have determined that you are at least qualified to close the deal you are inquiring about.

As you have probably discerned by now, brokers can both facilitate as well as represent a major hurdle to accessing deals. But you can turn that to your advantage. The fewer the buyers that cross the hurdle, the less competition you will have to deal with.

3.4   PACKAGING   YOURSELF   FOR   SUCCESS: YOUR BUYER INFORMATION PACKAGE

It is a good idea to have a standard package of information ready to send out, proactively or on request, when you are introducing yourself to brokers, sellers, or other parties in the acquisition process. A well-prepared information package can smooth the process by expediting the broker's task of determining your qualifications, and assuring sellers that you are serious about your proposal. Your information package will save you countless hours on the phone or at meetings explaining who you are and what you are looking for. Communicate this in different formats (document, spreadsheets, or presentation) and be ready to fax it, email it, or snail mail it.

Even better, have your own website where you can direct brokers and sellers. A well-presented website can speak volumes about your credibility and make it clear that you are a serious buyer.

Every Buyer Information Package should contain the details that will help other parties in the process determine who you are, what your qualifications are, and what you are looking for. The length of the Buyer Information Package will depend on the size and complexity of the business you are looking to acquire, and the amount of information you are comfortable with disclosing up-front. Most Buyer Information Packages are between one and three pages in length. Regardless of length, every package should contain the following sections:

1. Contact information

This section should include whatever information is required to reach you via mail, email, and phone.

2. Search criteria

The search criteria will let everyone know what you are looking for. The crisper your search criteria (see Chapter 2), the easier it will be to find the right business. Brokers will be able to help you look for deals if they know what you are looking for. Sellers who see it will recognize that they are in your target market.

3. Financial qualifications

Sellers and brokers are very forthright about financial qualifications. You either have the money, or you don't. The seller will bare his personal financial data (in the form of his company) to you. You will need to do the same. For the Buyer Information Package, a quick sketch of your financial situation should suffice. You should be ready to provide backup information in the form of bank statements, broker statements, and other evidence, if requested. When such private documents are requested, it is perfectly acceptable (and recommended) to black out the account numbers or your Social Security number, as long as your name and address are on the document.

4. Biographical sketch

Your biographical sketch will let other parties know that you are professionally qualified to run the business. The seller will likely have a stake in the business even after selling it to you, in the form of seller financing or even a minority equity stake, and will want to know that you have what it takes to succeed. While you don't have to provide a full resume at this stage, the seller will want to see a sketch that will convince everyone in the process that you are a real buyer. We recently saw a potential buyer bidding for a multimillion dollar transport company that was in need of a turnaround and subject to significant government regulation. The buyer did not have experience in managing turnarounds or in dealing with extensively regulated industries. In spite of bidding the highest, this buyer didn't win the deal because he could not convince the seller that he had the skills to manage the business after acquiring it.

3.5 CONVINCING SELLERS YOU ARE THE ONE

At some point you will have cleared the hurdles to reach sellers directly and will be making a bid for their business. You are likely to face competition here, as several people may have overcome the same hurdles to reach the seller directly. Several factors may be at work. For one, you may be in the dark about whether or not you have serious competition. Secondly, you have arrived at an appropriate deal structure and price, as per your calculations. (We will discuss more on this in Chapters 9 and 11.) It is possible that your bid is not as high as that of one of your competitors, or that the bids are equal (very likely if your offer is equal to the asking price). It is also possible that your bid is below the threshold of what the seller views as his minimum price. How do you convince sellers to accept your bid versus an equal or potentially more attractive alternative? How do you convince sellers that your bid offers more value than the financial tag attached to it?

1. Always deliver what you promise

Always deliver what you promise, whether it's a return phone call, documents, or a follow-up on a specific issue. Sellers will watch keenly for your level of commitment, even on seemingly inconsequential details. If you consistently keep to your word, sellers are more inclined to believe that you can deliver on the larger issues as well (like closing the deal on time and creating success with the business after the deal is closed).

2. Be polite and personable

Some people are easier to deal with than others, and they are the ones that people gravitate toward in their interactions. You don't want to give that broker a reason not to call you back, or to worry about introducing you to a client. Don't be smarmy or superficial; just be your usual pleasant self.

3. Be reasonable

Don't make unreasonable demands of the seller. We are not in a no-holds-barred battle and need not wrestle on every issue. Get what you need, but be reasonable about what you ask for. We know one buyer who prided himself on being a tough negotiator and beat down the seller on every issue. He never closed a deal in the eighteen months he looked. There was never a shortage of deals, but no one took him seriously because he gained a reputation for being unreasonable.

4. Be persistent

If the seller or broker didn't return your call, call again. If the seller accepted another offer, call in a week's time to see how it's going. Keep the attempts at communication going. The people you are trying to reach are very busy and you are likely to require more than one try to reach them. Not every deal closes. In fact, anecdotal evidence suggests that at least one-third to one-half don't. When a deal falls through and leaves the seller back at the beginning, he will almost always contact the other buyers who expressed interest, to see if he can make a sale without having to start the entire process over from scratch. At this point, the seller has often "spent the money" mentally and will be looking for a quick close with someone he thinks can be relied on to execute the transaction. If you have laid the proper groundwork in your previous interactions with the seller, you will be in a great position to close the deal.

5. Communicate your key messages

Above all, make sure that the seller understands that:

❖ You are financially qualified to do the deal
❖ You are serious about the deal
❖ You have the experience and background to be successful with the business
❖ You can close the deal quickly

Chapter 4

Building Your Advisory Team

In this chapter, we will cover:
* Why you need an advisory team
* The role of advisors
* Choosing your advisors
* Using your advisors
* Figure 4.1 The Need for a Search Broker
* Figure 4.2 Sample Advisor Introduction
* Figure 4.3 Sample Advisor Questions

4.1 WHY DO YOU NEED AN ADVISORY TEAM?

People often say, "Acquisition is a team sport." Like many other adages, this is true at least part of the time.

The issues and questions that may arise during your search, and particularly during the negotiation and closing stages of the deal, may test your expertise and experience. These issues usually crop up in legal and accounting areas, but are not uncommon in the areas like real estate, marketing, human resources, information technology, finance, and taxation. In addition, there will be many industry-specific issues to sort out, unless you are buying into an industry where you already have significant experience.

Answering the questions that come up during the course of your acquisition will determine the success or failure of your new business.

We recently witnessed an attempted acquisition of a large Eastern freight business. The deal looked good and the numbers lined up well. The deal was a little on the tight side, but had enough margin to cover most foreseeable events, including the requisite capital expenditure for new vehicles. However, the buyer was new to the trucking industry and did not have the expertise to accurately assess the condition of the current fleet of vehicles. On our advice, the buyer brought in an experienced fleet manager with a team and performed a thorough mechanical inspection of the entire fleet. The team found that 30 percent of the fleet would need to be replaced three years earlier than forecast by the current owner, and three years earlier than the buyer had planned for in his pro forma cash flow. The resulting impact on the buyer's cash flow projection was enough to create a negative cash flow for the first two years of operation. The buyer backed out of the deal immediately, saving himself hundreds of thousands of dollars in unexpected capital expenditure. The fleet inspection, which cost the buyer less than $5,000, turned out to be the best investment he could have made. The buyer, now a big believer in a solid team of advisors, went on to make a very successful acquisition in the industrial tooling business.

As the above example illustrates, it is important to have a team of advisors helping with the acquisition process. However, the team can only provide advice using professional judgment and based on input. But remember, the buck stops with you.

You still need to call the shots. Your team members may be enthusiastic and dedicated, but they are offering a professional service and get paid whether your deal is successful or not. The stakes are entirely different.

In a nutshell, it may be a team sport, but it is your hard-earned money that fuels it.

4.2   THE ROLE OF ADVISORS

1. The accountant

The accountant can help in a number of ways. It is important to clearly define your expectations from accountants. Accountants can assist in analyzing historical financial statements, preparing pro forma financial models, valuing the business, and executing your due diligence plan. The accountant will also help to structure the deal in a tax-efficient way and to determine the effect of taxes after the deal.

Your relationship with your accountant will often drive how much you utilize him. It is ideal if you have an informal arrangement where you can solicit his opinion on an issue without him making a research project out of it. A quick check with your accountant can often save hours of time and unnecessary expense.

Accountants are useful as a sounding board, especially in doing a first pass prioritization of potential candidates during the search phase of your business purchase. Say, for example, that you have identified twelve potential acquisition targets. You have done a first pass analysis and disqualified eight targets. If you send the remaining four to your accountant and ask his first reaction, he will likely see red flags that you would find only after several hours of research (if not, question your choice of advisor). His preliminary opinion, combined with your own judgment, will allow you to quickly zero in on the most attractive candidate.

You will probably rely heavily on your accountant for assistance if you are not familiar with the intricacies of company valuation. Companies for sale usually come with an asking price, and sometimes a valuation by a third party. These are the seller's numbers. You need to arrive at your own price independent of the seller, and your accountant is the person on your team who can help with this.

Your accountant can also validate the tax implications of your proposed business as you structure the deal, either as a Letter of Intent or as a Purchase Agreement. Failure to consult with an accountant regarding tax implications of a deal structure can be the difference between making and breaking the deal. So, make sure you seek tax advice from an expert before you lock on a structure.

You will need to carefully assess how to use your accountant advisor when the Purchase Agreement is signed and the due diligence phase is beginning. You can expect a very large bill at the end of the project if you use him for a complete audit of the company. Usually, full-scale audits are justified only if a deal is priced at ten to twenty million dollars or above. After reading this book, you will be able to determine the most critical issues for the accountant to focus on and for you to spend your money on, based on your expertise and the condition of the books of the target company. Your accountant can help you decide where his time would be best utilized.

If you have chosen your advisor well, he will likely continue as your company accountant after the deal is complete.

This should be an easy decision to make once you have had the chance to see him in action during the deal phase.

2. The lawyer

A good lawyer is essential to keeping yourself and your new business out of trouble and for guarding against unforeseen and unwanted liabilities or costs. The key role of the lawyer is to ensure that the contract has what you want, and that you understand all of it. He is your translator from legalese to English and back again. He can steer you away from deal structures that wouldn't stand up in court, and help you ascertain the legal status and potential liabilities of the company during due diligence. A good lawyer is essential to the business purchase process. We strongly advise against proceeding without one.

A mediocre or bad lawyer, on the other hand, can quickly destroy a deal and cost you a lot of money in the process. In our process, we tend to categorize lawyers as either "Dealmakers" or "Dealbreakers." Dealmakers will find ways around obstacles. They will find a way to make the deal happen that leaves their client fully protected, or at least acutely aware of the type and level of risk he or she is taking on. Dealbreakers kill most of the deals they work on by raising multiple objections and pointing out problems, but never providing solutions or only providing solutions that are unacceptable to the seller. Asking a lawyer how many deals he has been involved in and how many of them were closed is usually a good indicator of how he operates. You will still need to do your homework and rely on your intuition and contacts to get the real answer on this. We recommend you do this before you enter the deal. Once you're in the middle of a deal, it's too late to back away.

Lawyers can help during the search phase by providing leads to potential acquisitions. The company lawyer is usually among the first to know when a company may be for sale. Mid-sized firms focused on the local market will often use seminars on "how to sell a business" as part of their ongoing marketing and outreach programs. These firms will have the names of the attendees of those programs who are, presumably, interested in selling their businesses.

The first step in the purchase process will be a Letter of Intent (LOI). LOIs are generally simple documents ranging from one page to four pages. (For more about Letters of Intent, see Chapter 13.) LOIs are generally nonbinding, but will set the tone and parameters for your Purchase Agreement. It is important that the LOI accurately reflects your intentions. A lawyer should write or at least review your LOI. Your lawyer may suggest several points to add to the text of the LOI, but it will be up to you to strike a balance between what you want and what the seller will accept. Some issues will simply be nonnegotiable for the seller. Other issues may be best left until later in the negotiation process. (For more on negotiating, see Chapter 12: The Reality of Negotiating a Deal.)

You will be ready to move into the Purchase Agreement stage after you have agreed on general terms through the LOI. This is where your legal advisor will be most involved. Unlike the LOI, a Purchase Agreement is a binding contract. You do not want to find out down the road that you have forgotten to include a key clause in the document, or misinterpreted a clause that will cost you a pretty penny. Get your lawyer involved early in the process and keep him involved.

Your lawyer's involvement during the due diligence process will depend largely on the type, size, and form of purchase.

Some businesses will have specific legal issues that need to be investigated. A larger deal will generally require more legal due diligence than a small deal. A corporate or stock sale will usually require significantly more legal due diligence than an asset purchase. We will discuss in more detail the different legal forms of purchase in Chapter 15: Choosing a Legal Form.

The experience you have with your lawyer during the purchase of your business will help you determine if you should engage him as your company attorney once the deal is struck.

3. Roles of other advisors

Advisors, other than accountants and lawyers, are generally used if there is a specific need. The other most commonly used advisors are Business Brokers and Real Estate Agents.

You will encounter many business brokers in your search for a company to buy. These brokers are representing sellers. Some buyers find it useful to engage a broker to locate a business or to help them through the acquisition process. Most brokers are in business to sell businesses and are of limited use in proactively finding a business. But there are exceptions, and in some instances a broker can be indispensable.

A business purchase can benefit from the input and assistance of a good real estate agent in several ways. Larger deals will sometimes include real estate in the purchase price, and you will need to determine the approximate value of the parcel before making an offer. In this situation, you will want to follow up the due diligence phase with a formal real estate appraisal. For a quick estimate, turn to the agent for an approximate value of the piece of real estate based on comparable sales.

Another instance where a real estate agent is required is in the purchase of a retail business. The location is a key determinant of the success of a retail business. The location of the business may be leased or owned, but knowing the desirability of the location will be critical in helping you assess the overall attractiveness of the business.

4.3   CHOOSING YOUR ADVISORS

You want to choose your accountant and lawyer before becoming seriously involved with your first prospect. It would be disastrous to find the perfect acquisition, and then have it snatched away by another buyer because you didn't have an accountant or a lawyer yet. Your other advisors can be found as and when you need them.

You may already have an advisor that you intend to use. If so, make an informed decision on whether he really meets all your criteria, or if he is merely convenient.

If you're involved in an active search for an advisor, you will need to go through the process of identifying a number of candidates and narrowing it down to your top choice(s). Your initial inquiries should focus on the reputation of prospects. Naturally, one of the best places to start is with people you already know. Do they know somebody they think is great? Do they know somebody who has extensive experience working with accountants or lawyers that you could speak to? If your basic networking needs to be supplemented, consult with local trade organizations for the industries you're targeting, or a professional directory such as *The National Society of Public Accountants Membership Directory* or the local Bar Association.

Once you have several prospects (plan on at least three or four of each), schedule a time to meet them face-to-face. When you call to schedule an appointment, be prepared to give a short overview of the reason for your call and the source from which you got the advisor's name. You do not want to choose an accountant (or any other advisor) who doesn't have time to meet with you and discuss your business. Such advisors will not have time to provide a high level of service during the acquisition phase of your business purchase.

Usually, there is no charge for the initial meeting. Make it clear to the advisor that this is an informational interview, which may or may not lead to a business relationship. Confirm that he is not planning on charging you for the meeting before you actually meet him. The issue is not the charge for an hour of a lawyer's or an accountant's time, or your capacity to bear that cost. The larger concern is that an advisor who wants to bill you for the privilege of introducing himself to you is likely to nickel-and-dime you every step of the way during the process. That is not what you want or need on your advisory team. You want someone who will look at your business purchase as the beginning of a long-term relationship and will extend to you the necessary professional courtesies.

Repeat your brief overview of who you are and what you are doing in the face-to-face meeting. Start by asking the accountant some fairly open-ended questions about his background and the background of his firm. Narrow down to topics that will help you determine if he is the right fit for your particular needs, such as his experience in specific industries, average client size, or number of acquisition deals done. We always come prepared with two or three in-depth questions that touch on industry-specific or process-specific issues. These questions can help you quickly assess how flexible he will be about answering questions off the cuff and how rapidly he thinks on his feet.

4.4   USING YOUR ADVISORS

You may have built a world-class team of advisors, but they are as good as your ability to manage them. For each advisor, make sure to use the following:

1. Deliverables list: Every advisor should have a clear list of the deliverables he is responsible for. Don't rely on verbal communications. If you have a conversation over the phone, then follow up with an email detailing what has been agreed upon during the conversation. Be specific about the "what" and "when" of deliverables.

2. Progress updates: Ask that each key advisor update you once a week on his progress. This is easier if you can agree on a set day and time for the weekly update up-front. Check the progress against the timelines agreed upon. When you are in the negotiation process, you may need daily updates. Speak to your advisor about the frequency of updates. You want a time span that is long enough for him to get significant work done, but not so long that you feel left in the dark.

3. Quality control: You will get better quality work from your advisors if they know you will challenge them on it. You don't need to be aggressive, and it's better not to be. But you should review all documents they produce and ask questions. They know you care when they hear you ask serious questions.

4. Cost control: Remember that you are paying by the hour for the services of your advisors. Keep track of how much time they estimate for the items on the deliverables list and how much time they actually spent on them.

Chapter 5

Finding a Business

In this chapter, we will cover:
* ❋ The process of finding a business
* ❋ The small business market
* ❋ Business brokers
* ❋ Networking
* ❋ Dialing for dollars
* ❋ Making a plan

You have decided to buy a business. You have set your goals and identified the location, the type of business, and the size of business you want. You have created a team of advisors to help you through the process. Now, you are all set to start the hunt.

5.1   THE PROCESS

Businesses are bought and sold in almost the same way as you buy or sell a house. The business broker serves the same purpose as the residential real estate agent and is typically paid by the seller out of funds available at closing the deal. Banks and other lending institutions will loan you money. The Small Business Administration (SBA) sometimes serves as the guarantor of the money, a role similar to that of the Veterans Administration (VA) or Federal Housing Authority (FHA) in a house purchase. Escrow companies serve the same purposes as in a home sale: they act as a neutral third party, hold the money, and make sure that the terms and conditions of the sales agreement are met, and that everyone gets the money that is due.

There are some differences, however, particularly in the front end of the process, when you are trying to find a business:

❖ There is no Multiple Listing Service (MLS) for businesses. There are websites you can search, which we will cover below, but there is no single, organized, regional MLS used by every business broker.

❖ Typically, there will only be one business broker involved in a transaction, and he or she clearly represents the seller. Many business brokers make you, as the buyer, sign a document stating that you understand the broker represents only the seller. Interfacing with a business broker is covered below as well.

❖ You, as the buyer, may engage a business broker to help with the search or the negotiation of the deal, but it will probably be at your expense. Some brokers will "co-op" and pay a buyer's broker out of the seller's fee, but this is not the standard practice as it is with home sales.

❖ Do not expect to see a "business for sale" sign while driving down the street. Most sellers do not want their customers, employees, or competitors to have any idea they are selling the business.

5.2   THE MARKET

There are a lot fewer businesses for sale than houses. Most small businesses for sale are franchises or retail operations, and are available for less than a million dollars. BizBuySell (www. bizbuysell.com), at the time of writing this book, lists 197 businesses for sale in San Diego below a $1 million asking price, and thirteen businesses for sale at over $1 million. (By way of contrast, Realtor.Com [www.realtor.com] lists almost 7,000 houses for sale in San Diego.) The prices range from $25,000 for an Internet-based business to $7.5 million for an entertainment center with real estate.

There are larger businesses for sale as well. Larger businesses are typically sold through investment banks, using a totally different process that we will not cover. You may, however, run into a small investment bank or business broker selling a division of a larger company that qualifies as a small business. This, however, is a rare scenario.

Be prepared to work hard to find the perfect business, since the market is so small and there is no single list of available businesses like the MLS.

5.3   BUSINESS BROKERS

The search for a business begins with business brokers. The primary purpose of the business broker is to match a qualified buyer with a seller. The other functions of the business broker will be discussed in the appropriate chapters that follow.

Business brokers get listings in the same way that real estate agents get home listings. They advertise on the Internet and in the yellow pages. They network with lawyers, accountants, and others that may have a relationship with a small business owner who is thinking of selling. They also cold-call businesses to see if the owner might be interested in selling. They advertise those businesses on the Internet through their own website and industry sites like BizBuySell.

So, how do you find a business broker? There are primarily two approaches to finding a business broker: targeted and shotgun.

In the targeted approach, you search the websites that put up business for sale listings and find brokers who have listings that match your goals and selection criteria. This approach works best if the geographic requirements are fairly broad and it would be impractical to meet with all the business brokers that cover the area.

In the shotgun approach, you meet with every broker in the geographic area of interest. You have two goals with these meetings. First, to see if the broker already has a business for sale that matches your search criteria. Second, you need to get in his or her "rolodex," so that he or she will call you first if he or she does get a listing. Most areas have many more buyers than sellers. The business for sale may never show up on the Internet because the broker can sell it directly from the rolodex and avoid the cost and effort to list it. You need access to these unadvertised businesses, as they are usually the best opportunities.

The business broker wants to ensure that you are a qualified buyer. The more qualified you are, the more likely you will get the first call. To be considered as qualified, you need to be flush with funds or have access to adequate money. Business brokers usually have you fill out a buyer profile that often includes a personal financial statement. The greater your liquid assets, the more likely you will get a call when a new business listing becomes available.

You are selling yourself to the broker. Can you run a business? Can you make a decision? Are you serious about buying a business, or merely testing the waters? A resume can be very helpful convincing a business broker that you are serious.

The business broker needs to understand your search criteria as well. The more information about industry, size, complexity, and geographic location you provide to the business broker, the more likely he or she will present you with opportunities of interest.

Business brokers prepare an offering prospectus (we will discuss further the offering prospectus in a later chapter). To get the offering prospectus, you will have to sign a "non-disclosure agreement" (NDA) or confidentiality agreement for every business you investigate. We have yet to deal with a business broker who offers a generic or blanket NDA. Be prepared to sign a bunch of NDAs.

Typically, you will get only very general, unspecific information about the business until the NDA is signed. Usually, you will get the following information prior to signing the NDA:

- ❖ Industry ranging from very general (manufacturing) to specific (Chinese restaurant)
- ❖ Location ranging from geographic area (Midwest) to city
- ❖ Sales price, although some brokers like to say "call"
- ❖ Gross sales
- ❖ Adjusted cash flow ranging from specific to vague ($1M+)
- ❖ Included real estate, number of employees, years in business, etc.
- ❖ Reason for selling

The listing sales price needs to be interpreted carefully. Brokers tell us that businesses typically sell at about 90–95 percent of the listing price. We are not so sure of this statistic. We have had offers accepted at less than 75 percent of the listing price, and had the price go up to 20 percent above the listing price during negotiations. Usually, the sale price is whatever the owner is willing to sell for at that moment. The sale price will depend on many factors, including how long the business has been for sale and the financing terms. Do not be afraid to go after a business even if the price looks beyond your limit. All the owner can say is no.

We also need to talk about the stated "reason for selling." It would be great if you knew exactly why the business was being sold, but that may not always happen. Some reasons (divorce, death, illness, and moving out of the area) are fairly straightforward. Other reasons, including "pursuing other business interests" and retiring (if the owner is in his/her early forties) should make you very nervous. Be careful if the business is suddenly shown as very profitable, way beyond what you expect from the recent history of the business. Sellers try to get the absolute maximum value for the business, but do not necessarily want to tell you that. We looked at a cyclic, distribution-related business where the real reason that the owner was selling was that the market was getting soft! The owner had cut expenses (including his benefits) to make the cash flow look better. The listing reason for sale was "other business interests." The business was priced based on the most recent results. Do not blame the business broker. Brokers rely on the owners to provide accurate information, and go by what the owners tell them. Caveat emptor!

Broker Internet listings give you just enough information to get you interested, but not enough so that you can identify the specific business. The broker has to protect the seller so that the customers, employees, and competitors do not know the specific business is for sale. They also protect their fee by ensuring you cannot go directly to the seller, bypassing them. Most NDAs include a non-circumvention agreement that prevents a buyer from dealing directly with the seller without the broker.

The listing information available prior to signing an NDA should be enough to do a first prioritization of available businesses. Expect to eliminate 90 percent or more of the businesses available for sale, due to price, location, industry, or other factors that do not meet the criteria you established for a business to buy.

Business brokers typically do not get paid until the deal closes. Their fee is usually in the range of 3–10 percent or more, depending on the size of the business and the services they delivered.

You can engage a business broker to help you find and buy a business. For example, suppose you already owned a business and wanted to buy a smaller competitor. The business broker could approach the potential seller anonymously without tipping off your intent.

A broker can also canvass an area for businesses that meet your criteria. Starting with the yellow pages or a Dun and Bradstreet listing, the broker would call the businesses that meet your criteria. This can be done on a fee or a contingency basis.

5.4   NETWORKING

Do you know someone who might know of a business for sale? Lawyers, accountants, and bankers are often useful sources of information about businesses that might be for sale but are not listed with a business broker. They hear about business opportunities in the normal course of their business, sometimes even months before the business is listed for sale. It never hurts to be first in line. It never hurts to ask around.

5.5 DIALING FOR DOLLARS

Dialing for dollars is the do-it-yourself approach. Open the yellow pages to the appropriate listing and call all the businesses listed. Make a script and ask to speak to the owner or manager. Tell them you are researching companies in their business and have a few questions. People will normally tell you the size of the company (number of employees, number of trucks, etc.) and how long the company has been in business because you might be a future customer. They will usually clarify the scope of business services or geographic coverage as well. If the business seems to fit your criteria, you can contact the owner directly or indirectly (via a business broker) and explore the opportunity for a sale.

5.6 MAKING AND IMPLEMENTING A PLAN

The right business does not just fall in your lap. You need a plan to find the right business. We call this process "filling the funnel," because you will rarely, if ever, look at only one business. You need to make a list of candidates, narrow the list, and re-fill the funnel. We continue to look for businesses even after we have a letter of intent or are in due diligence. It is common knowledge that one-half of all deals that enter due diligence will never close, for one reason or another. The two most common reasons: failure to acquire financing and "issues" with the company books and records. We will cover these issues in more detail later.

Search the websites (national, regional, and broker-specific) weekly. Remember, you want to be first in line.

Keep records of the businesses you find, including the basic financial information. Try to understand and record why you decided not to pursue an opportunity, so that you learn from the process. What did you look at and why did you pass? If a business is still for sale months after you passed on it for price, maybe the price has become negotiable. You may want to have another go at it. Data is your friend.

Keep a list of all the business brokers you contact and the disposition of each contact. Did you sign an NDA and provide personal financial information? When was your last contact? You will need to contact each broker at least every three months, since you cannot count on them calling you. This callback process has frequently turned up opportunities for us. The brokers will not know if you have already bought a business or have altered you criteria in the interim unless you tell them.

Keep a file of the selling prospectus for each business you investigate. Some owners or brokers will want them returned or destroyed. However, they can provide useful information, particularly if you are looking at multiple businesses in the same industry.

5.7   CONCLUSION

Get out there and fill the funnel. We like to have at least two, and not more than four, businesses under investigation at any time. Search the Internet and call the brokers. You will probably have to look at a lot of opportunities to find one to pursue. The hunt is as thrilling as the acquisition!

Chapter 6
A Word About the Selling Prospectus

In this chapter, we will cover:
* What a Selling Prospectus is
* What to expect
* What you should ask for
* What to watch out for

6.1   WHAT IS A SELLING PROSPECTUS?

The first step, after you locate a potential business acquisition, is to get more information in the form of a Selling Prospectus.

The Selling Prospectus goes by many names, depending on who you speak to. It may be referred to as the Business Overview, an Information Package, or simply as "Additional Information." Regardless of what it is called, you need it. The information contained in the Selling Prospectus should enable you to determine whether you should pursue the acquisition of the target business. The quality and completeness of the document can tell you a lot about the company and what to expect in a full-blown due diligence process.

The Selling Prospectus is the seller's document. It has been prepared to sell the company such that the seller gains the maximum benefit. You have to validate everything in the document, either through your own efforts or those of your advisory team, or through direct questioning of the seller during the due diligence phase.

6.2   WHAT TO EXPECT

There will be variations in the quality and completeness of prospectuses you receive from sellers or their brokers. In the case of smaller companies, you are likely to receive just the tax returns. For larger companies, you should expect to receive a full Selling Prospectus, with much of the additional information detailed in this chapter. However, you will soon realize that size of the company is not the most definitive predictor of the quality of the prospectus.

The quality of the seller's agent or broker plays a major role in the preparation of the Selling Prospectus. Most brokers use generic questionnaires and checklists to gather information from sellers. Many brokers simply repackage information they have received and do not bother to ask for or include any other relevant information. Some brokers pride themselves on putting together comprehensive prospectuses. They validate the information received from their clients and go to the trouble of gathering much of the other information that you will need to make a decision.

If you are looking at a company for sale that is not represented by a broker or any other agent, it is likely that you will receive just what you ask for. If that is the case, make a checklist of the "What You Should Ask For" items and send it to the seller to prepare before you proceed any further.

What you should expect, at a minimum, is three complete years of historical Balance Sheets and Income Statements, plus the most current year-to-date figures. You are better off just moving on to your next potential acquisition if a seller cannot provide these vital details. (For more on analyzing financial statements, see Chapter 7.)

6.3   WHAT YOU SHOULD ASK FOR

A target business might still interest you even after you receive a poorly prepared information package. In such cases, do not hesitate to ask for more information.

A well-prepared Selling Prospectus should include the following:

1. **Business overview**

A well-prepared overview will contain the highlights of:

❖   What products or services the company provides
❖   What geographic area it operates in
❖   The financial highlights of the company
❖   Major assets for sale along with the company, especially any real estate
❖   A history of the company
❖   The number of employees
❖   An indication of the seller's asking price
❖   Whether the sale is an asset purchase or a stock sale

2. **Reason for selling**

The reason for the sale of the business is the most important piece of due diligence in the purchase of a business. After all, why will the seller not keep the business if it is doing great? We'll discuss more on this issue in Chapter 8. But the

Selling Prospectus should clearly state the reason the business is for sale. You will find that some will make vague statements about "other business interests." Others will be more concrete, with statements like "divorce forces sale." It will help you enormously if you ask for a specific and well-defined reason.

3. Products or service

The products or services that the company offers should be clearly defined. The definition should be clear enough to help you identify and assess potential competition for the company. The revenue contributed by each product or service must be spelled out clearly. This will help you separate the duds from the blockbusters, and assess the firm's potential for the future.

4. Market and customers

Each market that the company participates in should be described in terms of overall size, growth, and major competitors. Information should be provided on trends specific to that market. A detailed analysis of the company's customer base, including the number of customers, the nature of the customers, the percentage of business from repeat business, and the level of customer concentration should be provided.

5. Competition

The top competitors of the company should be clearly listed. There should be at least the minimum amount of information required for you to follow up and perform your own investigation, if you wish, for each competitor.

6. Organization

The number of people employed by the company and their roles should be included in the information. For example, you will want to know how many people are out in the field and how many are in the main office in a simple sales-related company. The role of the seller in the operations of the company is particularly important, as this is a function that you, as the buyer, will need to fill, either yourself or by hiring a new person.

7. Real estate

It should be clearly mentioned if the value of any real estate that is part of the sale has been included in the quoted price or not. If the real estate is for sale, then the zoning, square footage, building type, and size should be provided in detail. If the real estate is not included in the sale, or is an optional part of the sale, the terms of the lease should be detailed, along with a description of the physical facilities.

8. Assets and equipment

The Selling Prospectus should include a listing of all the major assets and pieces of equipment. For example, if the company is a freight transportation company, then the list should communicate the number and type of vehicles owned, and any warehouse equipment used by the company.

9. Financial statements

The summary financial statements of the past three years should be included. Often, sellers will provide annualized financials for the current partial year or forecast numbers for future years. It is fine to include the current year and future year numbers, but these are not a substitute for the information you glean from the historical numbers.

10. Adjusted cash flow

If the business is being sold on the basis of Owner's Cash Flow, then any adjustment to Earning before Interest, Taxes, Depreciation, and Amortization (EBITDA) should be detailed here. Major adjustments usually fall into one of several categories: depreciation, salary of the owner, and other expenses. The types and sizes of the adjustments can provide insight into the quality of the company's cash flow.

11. Valuation

Valuations provided by the seller are understandably biased. You will be better prepared to argue your own case in the negotiation stage if you can understand the logic behind the valuation. For example, the seller may clearly state that he is asking for three times the cash flow, and you may later demonstrate that cash flow is actually lower than represented. In such situations, you will be in a much stronger position to press a reduction in price based on the seller's own stated logic.

6.4   WHAT TO WATCH OUT FOR

As we said at the beginning of this chapter: remember that the prospectus was prepared to sell the company. Your safest course of action should be dictated by skepticism. In other words, do not believe anything to be true until you have validated it.

There are two warning signs that we have seen as endemic to companies that falter under closer examination. Foremost among these is the inability to produce credible financial statements. If the seller cannot produce the historical statements, it is a sign that he either does not want you to see them or that he is disorganized to the point where he simply cannot produce them. In the former case, it's clearly a warning sign. In the latter, you will need to think hard about his ability to build and grow a business that you would want to buy.

Second on our list of watch outs is where the seller or his representative verbally asserts "facts" about the company, but is unable to produce corroborating documentation. Statements like "Cash flow is actually much higher than the financials show" or "The business just booked three new big contracts that will triple the size of the company next year" should be viewed with extreme skepticism until you are shown proof. If sellers make statements like these and then fail to back them up with documentary evidence, you are usually best off walking away from the deal. Enlightened cynicism may just win the day for you.

Chapter 7

Assessing the Business Financials

In this chapter, we will cover:
* What Cash and Accrual Accounting is
* What Historical Financial Statements are
* What Financial Ratios are
* What Pro Forma Financial Models are

Based on your personal business goals, you have chosen the type and location of business you want, built a team of advisors to help you through the process, and searched for the perfect business. You have also narrowed down your choices to a few businesses that interest you and have gone through the selling prospectus. Gear up to move on to the next step of evaluating the target business.

The seller, obviously, aims to sell the deal, and will work to convince potential buyers that this is the best business for them. Buyers would buy the argument, too, if they worked only with the information provided by the seller and the selling prospectus. However, it is in your best interests to objectively evaluate the business before you proceed further. An assessment of the business financials helps in determining the long-term success and the current health of the business. The exercise will also help you determine the price you should pay for the business.

Table 7.1: The Five Point Checklist to Assess the Business Financials
❖ The type of financial statement provided by the seller
❖ All income, assets, and liabilities
❖ Source of key numbers and business notes
❖ Profitability, solvency, and liquidity ratios
❖ Pro forma earnings, expense, and cash flow statements with the underlying assumptions

Using a computer spreadsheet program for the assessment helps, especially in building different scenarios. We recommend that you consult with your accountant even if you are comfortable assessing financial statements. We have seen clients miss out on some crucial information because they were intuitively attracted to the business. Besides, it never hurts to have a second opinion on the numbers.

7.1   CASH AND ACCRUAL ACCOUNTING

Accounts are usually prepared using one of two methods: cash accounting or accrual accounting. The financial statements you receive from the seller will be prepared using one of these two methods. The method of accounting the firm adopts can give an indication of the type of business. Typically, businesses that do not maintain inventory or provide credit, such as service industries and startup businesses, use the cash accounting method. In contrast, product industries and industries that provide credit use the accrual accounting method.

The cash accounting method is used by many small businesses because it is simple and easy to maintain. In this method, a transaction is recorded when it actually happens. A sale is recorded when cash is received, and an expense is recorded when the actual payment is made. For example, the business might have made a sale in 2006, but received payment only in 2007. The transaction, in this instance, is not recorded in the books until 2007, when the actual payment is received.

In accrual accounting, the actual transaction is recorded as and when it occurs, irrespective of whether payment is collected or made at that time. If the business makes a transaction in 2006, it will record the transaction in the books of 2006, regardless of when payment is actually made. The accrual method matches income and expenditure and provides a clear idea of the financial operations of a business for a given period.

Find out which of these methods the seller currently uses. There are certain disadvantages to the cash accounting method. For instance, accounts receivable or payable are not recorded until the payments are completed. The cash accounting method also does not record bad debts, accruals, or deferrals. Buyers need to exercise caution when the seller presents a financial statement prepared using the cash accounting method even though the business extends credit. We had a client who wanted to purchase a printing business that was up for sale. The client had visited the site and had several discussions with the seller. The financial history looked good, the inventory seemed up-to-date, sales were good, and there was a large customer database. Our client was happy that he had found what he wanted. A careful examination of the financials of the business revealed that the seller had provided our client with a statement based on the cash accounting method. We found that the seller usually extended credit to his customers, which was not reflected in the statement. Even more alarming was the fact that the chances of collecting most of these accounts receivables were very slim. Needless to say, the deal fell through. Be prepared to ask for additional information on accounts receivable and accounts payable.

7.2   HISTORICAL FINANCIAL STATEMENTS

The buyer can determine almost everything about the past, the present, and the future of a business by making a careful review of its historical financial statements. The completeness of financial statements will depend on the purpose for which they are prepared. If this purpose was a compilation, the accountant would use the numbers provided by the management and present them in the proper format. He or she will not verify the accuracy of these numbers. If the statement is drawn up for a review, the accountant will make some attempt to verify the accuracy of the numbers by checking some or all of them. However, the accountant will verify all the numbers if the statement is prepared for an audited financial statement.

Buyers should always verify the authenticity of the financial statement that the seller provides. Enlist the help of your accountant to look over the statement, even if the seller has provided you with an audited financial statement. Do not hesitate to ask the seller about key numbers, and the process of arriving at these numbers. If you do not receive clear and specific answers, it may be time for you to seek additional information or cut your losses.

The financial statement usually has four parts.

1. The income statement

The income statement provides an insight into all the activities of the business for the stated period. The income statement usually has five parts.

❖ Sales or revenue. This section will provide the dollar amount of products or services sold during the year.

❖ Cost of products or services. This part will provide the dollar amount it cost the business to make the products or to provide the services. Needless to say, the cost of products or services should not exceed the sales or revenue. The gross margin, which is the sales or revenue minus the cost of products sold, is the amount of money that is available to cover the costs of running the business.

❖ Operating expenditure. This is the dollar amount that is needed for the daily operation of the business not included in the cost of products or services section. This will include all administrative and sales expenses such as salaries, travel, commissions, etc.

❖ Financial expenses. This section provides details of the financing costs incurred by the business, including interest. Higher financial expenses should raise a red flag immediately.

❖ Net income and tax. This section will provide details of all tax paid by the business to date. This will give you an idea of how much tax you need to pay, and if all appropriate taxes have been paid. The net income is the money earned by the business after all expenses are accounted for; in other words, the sale or revenue dollar amount minus all expenses. You will want a business with a reasonably high net income, enough to justify your decision to buy the business.

2. The balance sheet

The balance sheet analyzes the relation between the total assets, the total liabilities, and the equity of the business. The balance sheet provides you with a snapshot of the business as it stands at the end of the fiscal year.

❖ Assets. The total assets of the business include the current assets and the long-term assets. Current assets—like inventory, accounts receivable, and securities—can be converted into cash within the next fiscal year. In contrast, it might not be possible to convert long-term assets like property or infrastructure into cash within the next fiscal year.

❖ Liabilities. The total liabilities of the business include both current and long-term liabilities. Current liabilities are all debts or expenses that have to be paid within the next fiscal year. Long-term liabilities will include debts such as long-term loans or leases that will not mature within the next fiscal year.

❖ Equity. The equity section will provide details of all investments into the company, including any earnings that the business has gained over the years.

Ask the seller to provide the balance sheets of the business, preferably for the past three years, or at least for one year. Review the balance sheet to see if there are any marked changes in the assets or liabilities over the past years. An increase in the total assets are good as a rule, but buyers should check to see if there are valid reasons for such an increase. Marked increases in the liabilities, especially over and above the assets, may indicate fiscal mismanagement and the extent of financial burden you may have to bear in the future. Financial figures should always be seen in the light of the characteristics and specific peculiarities of the industry in which the firm operates. For instance, some businesses, such as advertising agencies, may routinely spend before receiving payment from clients. We had a client who was exploring the option to purchase a marketing agency. A review of the balance sheet revealed a large difference between the revenue, accounts receivables, and accounts payables of the agency. The client was tempted to drop the deal, but then decided to talk to other people in the communications industry. He soon found that this was the norm for marketing agencies, since they often ran up significant expenses prior to receiving payment from clients.

Why are expenses at the current level? Can they be reduced without affecting quality or productivity? Trends in the equity will tell you what investors feel about the business.

3. The cash flow

The cash flow statement traces the movement of cash in and out of the business. Basically, the cash flow statement tells you the cash at the beginning of the fiscal year, the sources of cash, the use of cash for expenses, and the final balance at the end of the fiscal year.

A review the flow of cash helps determine the frequency of payments and receipts. Buyers new to the industry should check carefully for any cyclic or seasonal trends that signal the need for additional working capital. A chat with the seller on how he or she managed any shortfall of cash would certainly help. Make a note if you will need to use your personal funds or seek support from a financial institution.

4. The notes

Many buyers tend to gloss over the notes attached at the end of the financial statements. We say they are a must-read, as they explain the process used to derive the numbers in the statement. Buyers should use these notes to verify if appropriate assumptions and processes were used.

7.3   FINANCIAL RATIOS

Ratios that evaluate liquidity, profitability, and solvency can be used to assess financial statements. Liquidity ratios tell you about the availability of cash and the ability of the business to convert or liquidate its assets to get cash. Profitability ratios tell you if the business has efficiently used the money invested in it, and the return on investment. It is better to invest in businesses that have a higher profitability ratio. Solvency ratios will tell you if the business is able to repay debts when they are due.

Ratios will vary widely depending on the industry. Make sure you are comparing like companies when using ratio analysis.

Ratio	Calculation	Indicator
Liquidity Ratios		
Current Ratio	Current assets/current liabilities	Assets sufficient to cover existing liability
Liquidity Ratio	Cash and Cash equivalents/liabilities	Sufficient assets that can be liquidated fast
Days Receivables and Days Payables	Average days to receive or make payments	Indicates health of cash flow

Profitability Ratios		
Gross Profit Ratio	Gross profit/sales	Crude profitability of business
Net income to sales ratio	Net income/total sales	Profitability of business
Operating income to sales ratio	Income before taxes/ sales	Management of business
Return on assets ratio	(Net income plus interest)/total assets	Management of assets
Return on equity ratio	Net income/total equity	Management of investments into business
Solvency Ratios		
Debt to assets ratio	Total debt/total assets or capital	Management of assets
Debt to equity ratio	Total debt/total equity	Management of investments

There are several other ratios that you might want to analyze, like the interest coverage ratio that tells you if the business can make its interest payments on time, and the turnover ratio that tells you the movement of inventory through a business. Talk to your accountant to work out the relevant ratios for your target business.

7.4 PRO FORMA FINANCIAL MODELS

Pro forma financial statements show the expected future direction of the business. However, these are hypothetical statements that project the future of a business based on current and past performance, and do not reflect actual results. Therefore, their accuracy would depend very much on the assumptions used. For a more realistic picture, we recommend that you base the assumptions on the analysis of the historical financial statements and the relevant ratios.

Typically, buyers use the pro forma earnings statement to project future income. This is tricky, as they will need to review the underlying assumptions and the historical financial statements carefully. They also need to incorporate the effect of the changes they will make after assuming ownership of the business. These may include changes in inventory, marketing strategies, target customers, and many others. There is also the need to factor in external changes, like those in the external business environment, the price of consumables, and others in the analysis. How will these changes impact your business, specifically on the sale of goods or services? Document the assumptions used for each pro forma statement.

The pro forma expense statement helps in gauging the potential effect of measures addressing expenses. In other words, it offers insights into the impact of cost-cutting or cost-containing measures before they are actually implemented. As a buyer, look for areas where you can retain quality and productivity at lower costs. What is the impact of cost cutting or cost containment? Sometimes, there are costs associated with cost cutting. For instance, you may want to reduce the number of personnel running a particular function of the business. Your analysis might reveal that to do so, you may have to invest in overtime expenses or additional training.

A forecast of earnings and expenses naturally leads to the construction of a projected cash flow. This is the dollar amount the business generates after meeting all operating expenses, including depreciation and amortization, and the buyer's salary.

The creation of pro forma statements is usually accompanied by some sensitivity analysis. This is important, because these statements are created based on assumptions derived from research and historical financial statements. Also, you haven't yet actually worked on the business. There is always the possibility that the assumptions used are wrong, or that there is a pronounced change in the situation. Typically, the assumptions are varied, preferably one at a time, to explore potential impact on the business. You can also use the spreadsheet to perform a break-even analysis from the pro forma cash flow. This analysis will help you estimate the income you need from your business to break even.

Roll up your sleeves and get down to decoding those numbers. A careful review of the finances of your target business will indicate if you have a lemon on your hands. Our advice to you is to make the most of your team of advisors. They can help you sift through your choices and come up with the winner.

Chapter 8
Assessing the Non-Financial Issues

In this chapter, we will cover:
* What you should know about the seller
* What you should know about the business (the company, its employees, customers, equipment, and suppliers)
* What you should know about general industry conditions (the competition, technology, and regulatory issues)

You have reached a decision about the location, type, and size of the business you want. You have assessed the finances of the target business and you are now ready to move on to the next step.

A business is not only about finances. The non-financial aspects of a business are equally critical to its growth. Logically, the non-financial aspects of a business that does well financially should be great. For instance, consider a restaurant that is doing well financially. The business does well because it generates revenues and has many customers. The customers are certainly attracted by the product offered or its price. However, there are other aspects that also draw customers to the restaurant, such as the ambience, the service, and the location, among others. Therefore, it is important to be convinced that the non-financial aspects are in good shape before proceeding with the purchase.

8.1   THE SELLER

The seller has invested his or her time, efforts, and money into the business and can provide valuable information that you need before the purchase of the business. With the seller as your ally, it will be a lot easier to gather information about the trends, competition, employees, and potential risks.

However, this will not come on a platter. More often than not, the seller will provide only as much information as he feels is required. We have seen several cases where an interested buyer asked probing questions and got so much more information, which helped enormously in the decision-making process. Review the information carefully and ask for the additional details you need.

Asking the right questions and getting adequate answers from the seller is a difficult but necessary task. This is a two-way street, though. The seller will not be open to sharing information unless the buyer reciprocates in the same manner.

Two tricky pieces of information the buyer needs to get are the reason the business is up for sale and what the seller plans to do after the sale. Answers to these questions are sometimes apparent—the seller wishes to retire or needs to move on due to health reasons. More often than not, the answers are vague. Sellers may or may not be open to sharing the information. Importantly, check if they plan to open or invest in a competing business. While figuring out these answers, you might even find that the seller is interested in helping you find financing for the business. If he found you perfect for the sale, he might even be willing to partly finance the purchase of the business.

One buyer who recently purchased a manufacturing firm developed a very good rapport with the seller. He had a lot of questions to ask, but made sure that he was always sensitive to the feelings of the seller. The deal closed smoothly, and the seller made it a point to personally introduce the buyer to employees and key suppliers. What's more, the seller actually went out of his way to get the buyer a good deal from the suppliers. A good recommendation from the seller to employees, suppliers, and customers is always useful.

8.2   THE COMPANY

The reputation of a company often reflects the reputation of the owner. People bring their personal qualities into the way they run the business. We once investigated a distributor who had put up his business for sale. He was popular and went out of his way to make people feel comfortable. We also found that he was very flexible with documentation and negotiations, doing what was necessary, but without being rigid about it. It came as no surprise that he had a large clientele who were very satisfied with his services. Unfortunately, his business suffered from chronic low profitability for the same reasons. Don't be satisfied with surface answers. Dig deeply enough to get at the real situation.

Talk to the seller about the development and progress of the business. Visit your target business. Are there a lot of customers? What do customers feel about the business? What changes, if any, do you envisage? It may be necessary to renovate, increase inventory, or do other general updates to the business.

These changes will cost money and must be factored into the value of the business.

Buyers also need to choose the post-purchase ownership structure. Many take the current structure as a given, which is not so. The ownership-related questions that need to be asked are: What is the current ownership structure? What has been the impact of such a structure on the business? Is there a franchise agreement (if the business is a franchise)? Is there a franchise fee that needs to be paid?

Explore if there are any specific agreements with suppliers. Has the business offered any product warranties to customers? Review these agreements carefully to understand the impact on the business in the future. Sometimes, these agreements may throw up surprises long after the purchase of the business.

Most importantly, ensure that the company is complying with all regulations, including environmental laws.

Figure 8.1 Key considerations about the business

The reputation of the business

Potential changes in the business

The ownership structure of the business

Leases or other agreements and terms

Intellectual property rights

Compliance with appropriate regulations

8.3   EMPLOYEES

Some of the most complex and vital decisions that need to be made concern the current employees of the business. Are they to be retained, or is a new team required, or will the buyer prefer paring down the staff and running the business himself? These decisions are determined, in part, by your experience and confidence in running the business, as well as the competence of existing employees.

Information that the seller can provide includes the roles of each employee, specific job descriptions, and employee contracts. The buyer needs to know how much the current employees are being paid, and how many of them are needed for each critical function of the business. It may be necessary to add or reallocate people to other functions. Start drawing up plans for these changes even as you file away such information for future use.

Talk to the employees. What do they feel about the business? How involved are they in it? Do they play an active role in the management of the business? One buyer we know spent a couple of days in informal discussions with key employees before proceeding with the purchase. One of the key employees, who planned to leave the business, provided him with several insightful comments on the business. The buyer realized that the potential of the employee had not been optimally utilized and made plans to remedy this by reallocating responsibilities. This employee rapidly became the buyer's key manager.

It is important to assess if the employees will stay with the business after transfer of the ownership. What will interest them to continue with you? It would be tough to break in a completely new team soon after you buy the business. It would be a good idea to avoid doing this, unless you do not trust the capabilities of the existing employees.

The call to retain existing employees or key management during the transition phase is essentially yours to make. Retained personnel can guide you during the transition and provide some continuity for customers, who would prefer seeing familiar faces. The decision to retain employees is usually thought about early in the pre-purchase stages, because employees carry a lot of market intelligence and knowledge about the business and not all of this is documented. This knowledge often walks out with them when they leave.

The role of the seller as an employee also needs to be closely evaluated. How much day-to-day work is the seller really doing? Sellers often understate their current involvement in the business to make it less of an issue for the buyer. Observe the seller in the workplace to see how often the phone rings, how many people stop in to ask questions, etc. In most cases, the seller (as an employee) will need to be replaced by either the buyer, an existing employee or a new manager hired for that purpose. Make sure you know who will be doing the work and at what incremental cost (if any).

Figure 8.2 Key considerations about employees

Specific job descriptions and employee contracts

Payment for employees

Employees for each critical function of the business

Involvement of the employees in the management of the business

Retaining key employees

Seller as employee

8.4   CUSTOMERS

A business grows because there are customers. Buyers need to understand more about the customer base of the business they plan to buy. How large is the customer base? Are customers concentrated in one or more specific areas? How is the current customer base relative to the past years? This knowledge will help refine your marketing strategy and expand the existing customer base.

A key question the buyer needs to ask here is: does the business retain the loyalty of its old customers? Ask the seller for some data on repeat customers: what percentage of customers come back and how often, any documented customer feedback, any warranty claims, how many new customers come through referrals, and so on. Typically, there would be some specific customer incentives or agreements in place. Sometimes, customers finance part of the operations of the business. In such instances, they may seek a return on investment through the sale of specific products. The customer may even fix the price of such products. A careful review of any such agreements will help you get a fix on the obligations you will take on if you buy the business.

Our experience shows that, apart from the statistics and details, certain other broad questions also need to be asked. A big one is this: what do customers *feel* about the business? Are they satisfied with the business? Approached the right way, current customers can provide feedback which yields some good ideas on ways to improve the business.

8.5   EQUIPMENT

Equipment is likely to be a major part of the purchase, especially if the target is a product business. Service businesses, relying more on people, do not always deal with equipment.

Ask the seller for a detailed list of all equipment. Determine the function of each item on the list, including whether it is automated or manual. When was the equipment purchased? Check if the equipment has been completely paid for or if there is a lease agreement for it. Find out if the equipment is still under warranty and the terms of warranty, and if there is an Annual Maintenance Contract (AMC) for the equipment. It's important to determine whether the seller has paid the AMC and when the next payment is due.

Answers to the above questions will help you assess the need to replace or upgrade existing equipment, or even purchase new equipment. Take into account all the indirect costs associated with the equipment. For example, equipment that is to be operated manually has an associated cost of personnel. In other words, you need to pay people to run the machine, and invest in training people to run the machine well. Other variables, including the costs of consumables and other recurring costs of the equipment, are to be considered. What is the wear and tear on the equipment under normal circumstances? What is the annual depreciation?

In situations where the equipment is a vital part of the business, it is better to seek the help of a technical team to evaluate the existing equipment rather than rely on the word of the seller alone. A technical evaluation will offer you a professional opinion on the current status of the equipment. This will help you plan your cash flow better and make a more informed decision on the purchase of the business. The resultant savings are often much higher than the consultation fee paid for the technical evaluation.

Figure 8.3 Key considerations about equipment

Detailed equipment inventory

Forecasted capital expenditures

Warranty, annual maintenance contract and terms

Current market value, book value, depreciation

Running costs

Technical evaluation

8.6 SUPPLIERS

Obtain a list of current suppliers from the seller. What relationship does the seller have with each supplier? The seller can give you the inside story on each supplier—what each one supplies, and the terms and conditions of each. Will suppliers offer you the same terms that are currently being offered to the seller? Review any agreements, the terms of payment, and trade credits with existing suppliers. You might be able to negotiate better terms. Are there any outstanding payments to be made? No one wants a long line of suppliers waiting outside the door soon after a purchase.

Be particularly wary of "personal guarantees." The seller may have had to personally guarantee the suppliers' payments when starting the business. The suppliers may want the buyer—or even the seller—to continue these personal guarantees.

Figure 8.4 Key questions to ask about suppliers

List of suppliers

Terms or agreements with suppliers

Outstanding payments or receivables

Retaining suppliers

8.7 GENERAL INDUSTRY CONDITIONS

Returns on investment are an essential consideration in the purchase of a business. To achieve good returns, the business has to succeed and grow. Along with studying aspects internal to the specific business, also look at the prevailing conditions in the industry in which it operates. Collect information on the current demand, buying pattern, trends, seasonality, and so on. Is the industry growing or has it stagnated in recent years? Assess the potential strengths and weaknesses of the industry.

There may be emerging opportunities that can be leveraged to benefit. Are there any foreseeable risks or threats to the industry? These risks may arise from internal or external factors. The business environment may be evolving in a way that will impact operations and the potential for profit.

The seller has access to information about industry trends, and may be willing to share this information. The buyer will need to validate this information by either performing his own research or contracting an external agency to do it for him. Buying a business is a major decision, and you do not want to get stuck in an industry that is on a downslide.

8.8   COMPETITION

Competition is good for growth, but it pays to know the competition before buying the business. The seller can provide you with a list of competitors, and the relative strengths and weaknesses of each competitor.

Again, in addition to seller-provided information, conduct your own research. Scout for information on each competitor. Make an informed judgment of their capabilities, and how they may impact the business. This knowledge will help you refine your marketing strategy.

Competition sometimes leads to collaboration. It is possible to work with your competitor(s) for mutual benefit. For instance, you may pool together to negotiate better terms for common supplies or undertake larger contracts than either of you could take on individually.

8.9   TECHNOLOGY

Technology is changing at a rapid pace. As a result, users of dated technology face obsolescence and a bill for updates. This is not something a seller will tell a potential buyer readily. You may need the support of a technical advisor to help you on this one. Do you expect a foreseeable change in the business environment? Will the computer/software platform that supports the business support its continued growth? For how long?

8.10   REGULATORY ISSUES

There are regulations that are common across states, and then there are state-specific regulations. Research the regulations that apply to your business in your state. Talk to the seller regarding compliance to such regulations. There may be specific licenses that must be maintained to run the business. Find out if these have been obtained and the costs involved with renewals. Are there any zoning laws that you have to be aware of? The website of the U.S. Small Business Administration (www. sba.gov) provides many resources on regulatory issues.

Chapter 9
Deal Structure Is Everything

In this chapter, we will cover:
* What Asset Sales and Stock Sales are
* What Seller Financing is
* How to allocate Purchase Price
* What Consulting and Employment Agreements are

You have assessed the financial and non-financial aspects of the target business. So far, your assessment has been positive, and you are now ready to make an offer for the business. Before you do that, you need to turn to another facet of the process. There are legal and tax considerations to buying a business. The structure of a deal determines its future tax and legal liabilities. A well-structured deal will enhance the success of the acquisition.

Figure 9.1 Key considerations to structure the deal

Asset sale or stock sale

Terms of seller financing, including future involvement of seller with business (if any)

Allocation of price for each component of the business

9.1   ASSET SALES AND STOCK SALES

Sellers often prefer selling the stock of the business while buyers often prefer to purchase the assets. A choice has to be made between buying the assets or the stock of the target business.

When a buyer purchases the stock of the business, he technically buys everything the business owns, including the liabilities of the business. While he may not be held personally responsible for the past actions, the assets of the business are at risk for the seller's past actions. In addition, stock sales are almost universally tax advantaged for the seller.

The advantage in an asset sale is this: only the assets of the business are acquired, not its liabilities. The seller can liquidate liabilities using the proceeds of the sale of the business which he receives. Buyers will almost always insist on an asset sale to limit the liability from the seller's past actions and reduce their own tax bill.

Licenses, certifications, or existing contracts with customers and suppliers can, in some circumstances, make an asset sale impractical. One of our clients had certifications that would have taken a year or more and tens of thousands of dollars to acquire if the transaction had been an asset sale. The risks (to the buyer) of a stock sale were far outweighed by the business impact of losing the certifications, and a stock deal was completed.

9.2   SELLER FINANCING

The buyer wants to pay the lowest dollar amount to purchase the business. The seller, of course, wants to sell the business for the maximum dollar amount. It is time to negotiate.

You can arrive at common ground by carefully structuring the deal.

Having come this far in the deal, it would be safe to assume that the seller wants to sell the business as much as the buyer wants to buy it. Most sellers are willing to finance some part of the purchase so that the deal is closed fast. The seller may finance the deal by providing a loan on certain terms. The loan can be structured so that less money is paid up-front, with the remaining amount paid over a period of time or with a "balloon" payment after a certain number of years. The interest rate and the duration of the loan are negotiable. Sellers will obviously be interested in a high interest rate and a short duration. Be prepared to accept a reasonable interest rate that is not much higher than the prime lending rate if you want to clinch the deal. Sellers may also be interested in being a part of the future growth of the business. It is possible to interest the seller in a future share of profits in return for financing. This structure is often referred to as an "earn-out."

An earn-out is often structured so that if the business achieves certain financial objectives (usually cash flow) the seller receives an additional payment. The arrangement may be for multiple payments over several years. Earn-outs can be great for closing the price gap near the end of a difficult negotiation, or for creating a viable financing structure where the future profitability of the business is uncertain.

Buyers like earn-outs because they lower their risk—no performance, no payment. Sellers often like earn-outs because they can negotiate a share of the business' future earnings.

A carefully structured earn-out is also the best way to keep a seller actively involved after the sale has closed.

Look for different ways that can guarantee a win-win situation. Flexibility is as important as ensuring that you get a good deal. In most instances, a deal can be structured to satisfy the seller and the buyer.

9.3   ALLOCATION OF PURCHASE PRICE

The dollar amount the buyer offers for the business is not a number chosen out of the blue. Essentially, a dollar value is placed on all components of the business, including the customers, suppliers, assets, employees, products, or services, among others. The sum of all these components is the purchase price the buyer is willing to offer.

Sensible price allocation can help the buyer structure a deal to legally reduce his tax liability. Some expenses of the business qualify for tax deductions; for example, operating expenses, depreciation, and interest. For instance, consider that you are retaining the seller as a consultant after purchase and have also entered into a non-compete agreement with him. You agree to pay $75,000 for a non-compete agreement. The $75,000 can be amortized and the consulting fees can be shown as current expenses. This will help reduce the tax burden on the purchase. Try to allocate as much of the purchase price as possible to such items. This will reduce your future tax burden. However, ensure that you are complying with any state or federal tax laws that apply to the purchase and the business.

When you buy the assets, you are able to reassess the value of each. You can increase the value of assets if, at the time of the purchase, the book value of the assets is below the fair market value. This will help you get some tax benefits in the future; for example, through depreciation of the assets. Let us look at an example that illustrates this. Say, for instance, that you buy a business whose book value of the assets is $1,000,000. You do your research and find that the current fair market price for these assets amounts to $2,000,000. You can reassess the value of assets purchased as $2,000,000. If the assets have a life of five years in the normal course, you can depreciate these assets by an additional $200,000 each year. The depreciation decreases the tax profits of the business, and consequently the tax you have to pay.

There are transactions that do not offer tax benefits. For example, if you buy the stock of the company, the amount you pay for the stock will be based on the estimates of the owner. This will include the value of the stock plus any additional working capital. Usually, the buyer ends up paying more than the estimated value of the stock. This excess payment that is over the book value of the business will be considered as a goodwill transaction. Goodwill transactions are intangible assets and do not offer much in the way of tax benefits. We can illustrate this using the example given above. Consider a situation where you have not shown the reassessed value of the assets in your books. However, you have paid the seller $1,500,000 because you felt that you cut a deal below the fair market price. The $500,000 that you have paid in excess will be considered as goodwill and will not offer significant tax benefits.

These are some pointers, but we are not accountants. All the above considerations should be discussed with your accountant.

9.4 CONSULTING AND EMPLOYER AGREE-MENTS

You may or may not have the expertise or experience to manage your new acquisition. In any case, it will be useful to tap the experience and customer relationships of the seller. As we have mentioned before, the seller is often an invaluable ally, especially during the transition phase. The seller can smooth your introduction to the customers and suppliers, and to the employees.

How long do you want the seller to stick around? What should you offer the seller in order to do so? How do you formalize the arrangement so that there is no heartbreak at a later date? It is important to think through these operational issues before you buy the business, even though they may not appear to be essential to the purchase.

There are other equally good reasons to request the seller to stay on with the business, at least for a transition period. For one, you certainly do not want the seller to set up a competing business with the payout you give. Instead, you would like to see the seller involved with the business. Besides the guidance you receive, involvement of the seller will also indicate the confidence the seller has in the continued success of the business.

The seller can be an active manager in the business. The seller works for you, and you use his or her strengths to the maximum. You have to create well-defined job descriptions that detail what you expect from the seller. While you're at it, also consider the flip side of such an arrangement. Will the seller be interested in working under you? You will be the boss, and he or she will have to listen to your ideas on how to run a business that he or she has nurtured over the years. The potential for conflict is always there.

Next, how long do you want the seller to be with you? It depends on your confidence and comfort levels, and the interest of the seller. Ideally, aim for a short transition period. Of course, if it is mutually beneficial, you may consider keeping the seller as a full-time manager.

If you want the seller to work for you, talk to your lawyer, the seller, and his team, and draft an employment agreement. An agreement is essential even if you enjoy a great rapport with the seller. You do not want any unpleasant surprises later. The agreement should include details of the appointment, the responsibilities, compensation, confidentiality or non-disclosure clauses, and terms of termination or modification of the agreement. Your lawyer can advise you on additional clauses. The aim is to minimize your risk while providing maximum benefits for you and the seller.

Sometimes, you or the seller might not feel comfortable with an employee position. In such cases, you can consider offering the seller a consultancy position. You can take control of the business and make use of the expertise of the seller as necessary. Payments for consultancy offer tax benefits, too, so you have an added advantage. The consultancy agreement should list details of expectations or duties, compensation, confidentiality clauses, termination or modification of the agreement, severance, and other clauses. You may even insert a non-compete clause or have a separate non-compete agreement with the seller.

Think through the structure of the deal before you actually commit to the purchase. You have to work with the seller to get the best structure that benefits both of you. Be reasonable and try to arrive at some common ground. You do not want to discomfit the seller such that he or she walks away from the deal. Often, the dollar value for the experience of the seller is priceless. Think win-win.

Chapter 10
Financing the Deal

In this chapter, we will cover:
* How to estimate the financial need
* What the sources of funding are
* How to get the funds

10.1 ESTIMATING THE FINANCIAL NEED

We often see clients sold on the idea of owning a business who forget that a business needs a constant infusion of funds to keep running. The thrill of owning a business is great, but it's a good idea to estimate the expenses and the working capital before you buy one.

The working capital will include the accounts receivable (AR), the accounts payable (AP), and the inventory; in other words, the current assets and liabilities of the business. It is useful to understand the sources of working capital or the uses of funds to make better estimates of the operating cash flow of the business. For instance, if the business does well and revenue increases, it will need an increasing level of AR to fund that growth. Similarly, inventories and AP will also grow. Understanding the relationship between revenue and working capital is crucial to ensuring an adequate supply of cash to fuel your business growth.

Typical expenses for a business include rent, office supplies, maintenance, insurance, utilities, marketing, labor, and licenses. Businesses that produce a product will have other specific expenses related to the production process. The buyer will need to factor in these expenses while preparing the estimates. Existing capital equipment must be evaluated for age and remaining useful life to determine replacement capital equipment costs as well. Typically, service businesses need less cash, as the costs for material and equipment are low.

The buyer will need to have adequate cash for the equity investment. While there are no fixed rules for the down payment, a reasonable assumption would be 25 percent of the sale price. The size of the target business will, in part, determine the down payment and the financial support the buyer needs to buy the business.

You will need to find alternate sources of funding to cover the down payment. To secure the deal, you also need to show that you have adequate sources of working capital even after clearing the down payment.

10.2 SOURCES OF FUNDING

There is always money available for a sound business proposition. You just have to know where to find it. Typically, private players like banks, commercial lending institutions, private investment firms, or quasi-public sources like the SBA offer funds for the purchase of businesses. A common source of funds is the seller.

1. The Seller

In our experience, the seller is often your best bet for financing. Usually, sellers are willing to finance some part of the purchase price. It could be because the seller wishes to retain some stake in the business. He may want to be a part of its growth because he is convinced that the buyer is serious and can run the business successfully. He might also feel that by financing the deal, he will get the right price for his business. Even if he is not driven to remain a part of the business post sale, he is very likely to want to help you find financing simply because he wants to close the deal as quickly as possible.

2. Banks

The bank is often the first option that people explore when they need additional cash. Banks have money and are willing to lend to the right customer. But there is a caveat; they are usually wary of taking risks. So, you really need to sell your business proposition to get them on board.

There are different kinds of banks, and you have to carefully review the differences before you choose a particular bank. For example, savings banks will have more experience with consumer loans, while commercial banks will have more experience with business loans. Choose a bank that you are familiar with, one where you have done business before or one that a member of your advisory team can introduce you to. You can also consult a banking directory to get more information on banks.

3. Credit Unions

Employees or members of a company, or a labor union, may develop a financial institution focused on providing service to its members. These credit unions offer lower interest rates than banks and other lenders. The buyer can approach a credit union directly if there is one at the company where he works.

4. Finance Companies

Consumer finance companies are governed by the regulations related to small loans. These companies often provide small loans secured against collateral such as assets of the business. Consumer finance companies are very flexible about approving requests, and it is possible to get a loan even if your credit rating is poor. There is a catch, though. These companies charge very high interest rates, relative to bank or seller financing.

Commercial finance companies provide loans to purchase inventory or equipment, and focus on business loans. Like consumer finance companies, they charge high interest rates and are more flexible in approving requests for loans. They collateralize the debt and can seize your assets if you default on payments.

5. Small Business Investment Companies (SBICs)

The SBA licenses and operates the Small Business Investment Company (SBIC) under its guidelines. The SBICs are privately owned companies, but are chartered by the state in which they function. The SBICs can provide both loans and equity investments.

SBICs can be extremely flexible in structuring their lending and equity investments. They generally do not require personal guarantees. Rates are usually double what a bank would charge. For more information on SBICs, see http://www.sba.gov/aboutsba/sbaprograms/inv/index.html.

6. Investment Firms

Venture capital firms are sources of equity funds, but do not provide loans. Venture capitalists are driven by profits. Usually, they invest in businesses that have a potential for unusually high returns in a short period of time. They are also interested in businesses that provide options for early exit through sale of their interests in the business for a profit. Venture capitalists are committed investors who play an active role in the strategic management of your business.

Closed end investment firms are similar to venture capital firms, but with less money for investment. They will purchase stock of your company that they may, in turn, sell to private investors.

7. Corporate Capital Sources

Corporate capital sources will invest in the business in exchange for some form of ownership. The ownership may take the form of a complete purchase, where the corporation buys out the entire business. In such cases, the buyer will not retain any rights to the business. The corporation may explore partial ownership, purchasing a part of the stock of the business (similar to investment firms), or may explore joint ownership. In a joint ownership, you get to run the business while the corporation provides the capital and technical support. The corporation may also support a licensing agreement, where you retain control of the business but receive cash for work performed on a contract basis.

8. Employee Stock Ownership Plans

The buyer may also choose to sell stock directly to the current employees of the target business. He will lose a certain degree of control, similar to other equity arrangements, but will be sharing control with employees rather than outside investors who may be complete strangers—at best, indifferent, and at worst, detrimental to the growth of the business. Obviously, this will work only if the target business has employees that can be approached.

9. Private Investment Partnerships

These partnerships involve one or more members who will provide capital for the business. The partner(s) are passive investors, unlike venture capitalists, and do not play an active role in the strategic management of your business. These partnerships are generally local or regional arrangements. If there are active partnerships in your area, the best way to locate them is through your network of advisors.

10. U.S. Small Business Administration (SBA)

The U.S. SBA guarantees long-term loans to small businesses that are unable to obtain financing through normal lending channels. The SBA assesses the qualification of the business before guaranteeing the loan. Usually, the SBA guarantees 70–90 percent of the loan amount. The interest rates may be slightly higher, but will not exceed 2.75 percent more than the prime lending rate. There is a downside to SBA financing, however. The SBA often will place a lien on your personal assets, including your home, to guarantee the loan. SBA loans are the most common form of funding for business purchases.

You can contact the local district office of the SBA for guidance on the various programs. You can also visit its website (www.sba.gov) for online assistance.

Table 10.1 Funding Options

Funding Option	Availability	Type of Funding	Benefits/Limitations
Seller	High	Debt	Keeps seller involved. Can negotiate good repayment terms.
Bank	Moderate	Debt	Repayment terms may not be very flexible. Loans usually limited to 60–70% of tangible assets.
Credit Unions	Moderate	Debt	Lower interest rates than banks.
Finance Companies	High	Debt	Very fast, responsive. Requires tangible assets as collateral. Higher cost.
SBICs	Low	Debt/ Equity	Will structure flexible funding packages. No personal guarantee. High cost.
Investment Firms	Low	Equity/ Debt	Difficult to find and access.
Corporate Sources	Low	Equity	Lose some ownership of the business.

Funding Option	Availability	Type of Funding	Benefits/Limitations
Employee Stock Ownership Plans	Low	Equity	Potential employees might be interested, buyers stand to lose some control of business.
Private Investment Partnerships	Low	Equity/ Debt	Difficult to find and access.
SBA	Highest	Guarantor of Loan	Most common source. Strong personal guarantee required. Will lend more than traditional bank loan without collateral.

10.3   GETTING THE FUNDS

There is one common thread that runs through all the sources of financing that we discussed: the buyer has to sell the investment proposition to someone who has the money. To do so, he has to engage their attention and convince them that he is the best person to borrow their money. You have to convince the investor of your competence. You must demonstrate that you have collateral to offer, a clear source of repayment, and a good business plan. Be prepared to back each statement with documented evidence.

There is much to do once you have decided who to ask for the funds you need.

1. Prepare a comprehensive business plan

Most buyers we meet have a lot of ideas to make the business a success. We tell them that these ideas need to be translated into a business plan in order to secure the funding they need. The business plan should include:

- The amount and purpose of the loan: why do you want the loan?
- The uses and benefits of the loan: how will the money be used, and how will it benefit the business?
- The income projections and cash flow, preferably for three years, or at least one year: how do you see this infusion of funds affecting the cash flow?
- The expenditure statements of the past three years of the business.
- Management and staffing pattern of the business.
- Details of competitors, marketing, and pricing strategies.
- Collateral available: what collateral will you offer for the loan?
- Current personal financial statement.

The SBA website (www.sba.gov) offers guidance on preparing a good business plan.

2. Approach the Right Person

This is where the buyer's attention to detail and homework pays off. He needs to know who will make the decisions on requests for financing, as well as the lending limit. This is the amount of money that the lender can approve without sanction from any other authority. You do not want to put your best foot forward only to be directed elsewhere. You definitely don't want to bargain with the front office when the manager calls all the shots.

3. Be Realistic about your Financial Strength

A buyer's credibility is his biggest asset. The lender will verify every statement you make. Be prepared to provide documented evidence of every financial statement. If you state that you have collateral to offer, be prepared to show evidence. You lose credibility and potential lenders if you cannot back up your statements.

4. Research the Lender

This is a major business decision. The buyer needs to conduct a thorough background check of potential lenders or investors. The relationship with the lender or investor is long term, and you are better off with someone you are comfortable working with.

5. Be Prepared to Negotiate

Different lenders will charge different interest rates and fees. The term of the loan may also vary between lenders. Do not hesitate to negotiate for a reduction in rates or duration of the loan. At worst, the investor may say that the terms are not negotiable.

It will take time for the lender to approve a request for financing. It will take more time for money to actually change hands. This is the reason why the buyer needs to plan his financial needs in advance. Do not get discouraged if the lender turns down your plan. Try to understand what may have gone wrong. Ask the lender for feedback. Review your business plan with your accountant and lawyer. Work on rectifying any perceivable weakness in the plan. Try alternate sources of funding. Perseverance pays, especially if your business ideas are good.

Chapter 11

The Right Price

In this chapter, we will cover:
* What the Right Price is
* What Net Cash Flow is
* What Principal and Interest Coverage is
* What Discounted Cash Flow is
* What the market will bear

11.1 WHAT IS THE RIGHT PRICE?

You have chosen your target business and spent time structuring the right deal. You have made estimates of the cash you need to buy the business and have decided upon a financing option. You are now ready to make the offer. Naturally, you do not want to offer more than the value of the business. Besides, what you save in pricing, you could plough back into the business for additional profits.

We find that by the time buyers reach this point, they have started thinking of the business as their own. They have invested too much in terms of time, effort, and money to walk away from the deal—unless, of course, there is no other choice.

This is a blanket rule—understanding the assumptions behind estimations of price will help buyers negotiate a better deal. Remember, you are not here to undercut the seller, but to ensure that both of you gain the maximum from this deal. The seller is a future ally and you do not want to antagonize him or her. Your goal is to have a win-win situation.

Pricing is possibly the single most important factor in the entire deal. The buyer must leverage the collective wisdom of his team of advisors here; not only can they give him an objective view of things, they also have years of experience and have seen many more deals such as this one. Look at different scenarios and various methods of evaluation to arrive at a set of potentially reasonable numbers. As we said earlier, get another opinion on the numbers even if you are an expert.

11.2 NET CASH FLOW

We have discussed the calculation of net income (see Chapter 7 for more details). We can use the multiple method to estimate a net cash flow that will help to determine the right price for the business. Basically, the net adjusted cash flow of the business is multiplied by a market-driven number that is assumed to be appropriate. Although multiple methods are commonly used, they are subjective, since they depend on historical cash flows and rely on the observed multiple for similar businesses. Often, the source of the multiple is hearsay. The use of historical cash flows may not reflect external changes in the overall business environment.

The right price for the business can also be determined from the net income using a capitalization rate method. The method is similar to the multiple method and shares the same limitation of arbitrariness. The capitalization rate method is based on determining a target return to be earned from the price of the business. The net income is divided by the capitalization rate to arrive at the price of the business. For example, assume that the income of the business you wish to purchase is $1,000,000. Your research of the industry indicates that a capitalization rate of 20 percent, or 0.2, is reasonable. The price to offer for the business is then calculated as $1,000,000 divided by 0.2, which equals $5,000,000.

11.3   PRINCIPAL AND INTEREST COVERAGE

Even if he is enamored with the idea of owning the business, the buyer must determine its ability to pay its debt. In other words, he will want to review if the earnings and revenue from the business will be sufficient to pay the interest and at least part of the principal.

The Earnings before Interest, Taxes, Depreciation, and Amortization (EBITDA) is used to estimate the principal and interest (P&I) coverage. The P&I coverage is estimated as the ratio of EBITDA to expenses for interest. Depreciation and amortization are ignored for this estimation, because they are non-cash expenses that do not interfere with the ability of the business to pay its dues. Tax is not taken into consideration because the interest is paid before the tax on profits is paid. The payback period for the loan or debt is estimated as the ratio of the debt to EBITDA. The risk to the business is greater if the payback period is longer. However, the EBITDA is not a Generally Accepted Accounting Principle (GAAP) measure. The calculation of EBITDA may vary from business to business. You have to review the results carefully and form your own judgment. A more detailed discussion of EBITDA and the risks associated with its use can be found at http://en.wikipedia.org/wiki/EBITDA.

11.4 DISCOUNTED CASH FLOW

You are willing to pay a dollar amount to acquire the business today. Dollar values change over time. The dollar amount you pay today might be worth more than the same dollar amount in the future (the time value of money). The buyer has to determine what he should pay today, keeping in mind the possible devaluation of the dollar in the future. The discounted cash flow helps you do just that.

The discounted cash flow method uses future projections of cash flows and discounts the cash flows for each future year back to the current year. The discount rate is determined based on certain assumptions, including the risk of the business, the interest charged on debt, the returns expected on assets and equity, and the opportunity cost of capital.

Typically, buyers would consider different scenarios—what happens to the worth of the business if the seller continues to operate it, and what happens if you buy the business. The worth of the business may not change much, for good or for bad, if the buyer does not plan many changes to the business. However, it is more likely that he will make certain changes to it. As a result, there will be a change in the value of the business once he has made changes in its functioning. These changes could have a positive or an adverse impact on the business.

You will need to look at a worst-case scenario, a best-case scenario, and a status quo. Look for a price that justifies the business as it is worth under the seller's leadership.

Use the pro forma statements to project the financial results of the business for the next five years. Determine the annual growth rate and annual expense rate from the historical financial statements. Determine the non-cash expenses of the business. You can now estimate a projected net income for the business that can be discounted back to the time of purchasing it. Ensure that the discount rate you apply is appropriate for the risk profile of the business you are acquiring.

Of course, you need not offer the seller the discounted dollar amount. You can negotiate to buy the business for a lower price or at the actual market value.

11.5   WHAT THE MARKET WILL BEAR

The buyer has to determine the price that accurately reflects the value of the assets of the business if it were to sell on the open market today. The book value will give him an indication of what the business is worth, but he still needs to estimate the market value of the business. There is no "plug and play" approach one can use to determine the price that the market will bear. You need to look at different considerations for each asset of the business. For instance, a software development company may show poor annual returns as it develops the product. The market price for such a business may still be high, as the returns are expected to increase many times when the product hits the market.

Go back to the historical numbers. Review the accounts receivables (AR). Are there accounts receivables that are older than three months? Review the customers who have accounts receivables. What is their trend of repayment? Can you realistically expect to collect these ARs? Sometimes, you may have to offer a discount (based on the "something is better than nothing" principle) to collect the AR. Accounts receivables that do not stand a chance of being collected artificially inflate the value of the assets.

Review the inventory. You want to know the normal life span of the inventory, and if it is in active use. Are the products finished goods, raw materials, or products that are in different stages of completion? Review the terms of existing arrangements for renting or leasing equipment and facilities. Find out when these arrangements expire and what will happen if you have to renew them.

In fact, you do not have to buy all assets when you do an asset purchase. You can pare down the list to only those assets that are useful and are earning revenue for the business.

You will also want to consider the intangible assets of the company. It may be difficult to place a dollar value on such assets, but these can be priceless. For example, a business with a very good reputation and a large customer base is invaluable. Generally, buyers pay a goodwill price for such intangible assets.

The seller will tell you the listed value that includes a valuation of the tangible and intangible assets. You might actually end up saving a lot of money if you do your research well.

Chapter 12
The Reality of Negotiating a Deal

In this chapter, we will cover:
* How you can lock the deal early
* How you can own the process
* What some common traps and tactics are

By now, you have done a lot of research and are ready to acquire your target business. You know the structure of the sale you want, and have analyzed the financial and non-financial aspects to determine a price for the business. You also have better clarity about the financial options that are available to you.

However, the process of buying a business is not as simple as stating a price and closing the deal. The seller will have his or her own idea of the price, which is very likely to be different from the price you are willing to pay. Be prepared to negotiate the deal with the seller and his or her representatives. With a lot of luck, it could be short—but routinely, it is a longer process.

12.1 LOCK THE DEAL EARLY

The buyer is eager to lock the deal early and elbow aside the other potential buyers. The seller also prefers a quick settlement, and does not wish to get trapped in a long, drawn-out process.

While we would readily admit that most of the discussion is about the price, negotiations are not just about numbers. The negotiation process actually starts during the buyer's first interaction with the seller. We say this because the rapport developed with the seller is a very important part of the negotiation process. The buyer must start early and try to understand the seller better. Why is he or she selling the business? What drives him or her? How does he interact with customers or suppliers? Is she a tough negotiator, or open to some give and take? Try to gauge the alternatives open to the seller if he or she decides not to sell. You might not always be aware of other competitors, but negotiate assuming there are other equally interested buyers.

The seller will form a judgment based on the interactions with the buyer at each point of contact. Buyers have to continuously impress upon the seller that they are serious about the acquisition and capable of closing it. True, the seller would want the best price on offer, but money may not be the only criteria by which a sale is determined. Your research about the business, the information you share with the seller, the assumptions used to evaluate the business, the structure of the sale, and the ability to raise the necessary finances are all important considerations. We know a recent deal that involved the sale of a distribution business. The buyer liked what he saw and was keen to clinch the deal. Negotiations, however, stalled for some time on a technical evaluation of the equipment. The seller, through his previous interactions, felt that the buyer was procrastinating under the guise of collecting more information. He kept his options open with other interested buyers, and eventually informed the potential buyer that he had made the sale at a lower price to another buyer.

Buyers should have all the numbers at their fingertips. What is the optimum price for the business? What is the maximum price for the business? Buyers should understand the process of arriving at these numbers so that they can explain them on demand.

Buyers who recognize and understand the key considerations of the deal are more likely to settle it early. Any transaction will have areas that are considered non-negotiable and areas that are negotiable. Try to prioritize areas based on their relative importance. What are the non-negotiable areas from the buyer's perspective, as well as that of the seller? It is possible to develop an idea of these through research and interactions with the seller. You will save time and money if you have this information before the actual negotiation begins.

Deals fall through frequently simply because either the seller or the buyer takes a rigid stance. Be prepared to modify your style of negotiating based on the circumstances. Play soft on issues that are relatively unimportant and take a tougher stance on issues that are non-negotiable. The ultimate goal is to walk away with a win-win situation, so be flexible in your approach. If you have done well in observing and learning through your interactions and research, you would be able to anticipate the responses of the seller by this time. In fact, this should be your goal from the outset.

Make a list of possible questions or barriers from the perspective of the seller. Work out how you plan to solve these issues before you actually start the negotiation process. Remember, the better-prepared person has the edge during negotiations.

Buyers need to negotiate the issues objectively. For instance, the seller may be fixed on the purchase price and may not budge from it, even after hours of negotiations. Rather than allowing the negotiations to stall at this stage, you can try to find a way forward by structuring the payment terms to your advantage. You can request for a longer term to make the payment, or ask for a different purchase price allocation to your tax benefit or an earn-out that shifts some of the risks to the seller. Getting personal or taking issues personally at any point during the negotiation is a strict no-no. When in danger of losing focus, remind yourself that you really want to buy the business, but do not want to be saddled with the debts or woes of the seller.

Buyers are in good shape if the seller has agreed to sit and negotiate with them. At this point, sellers are looking for confirmation that they are making the right decisions for a reasonable price. Your research and preparation will allow you to provide solutions to any potential issues that may arise and will help you lock the deal early.

Table 12.1 Key considerations before you start negotiating
❖ Determine the range of price for the business
❖ Identify issues that are non-negotiable
❖ Determine how much negotiation is acceptable on other issues
❖ Prepare a list of potential issues you anticipate from the seller, and how you plan to resolve them

12.2   OWN THE PROCESS

It is better to be proactive rather than reactive during the negotiation process. The buyer is better placed to seal the deal if he has control over the process and can guide the direction of negotiations.

Typically, a seasoned buyer would move along the prioritized list of issues that he has prepared. The seller might jump the list, since he or she will have his or her own priorities. Spend time listening to the seller. You may have anticipated issues raised by the seller if you have prepared your brief well, and will have solutions to these issues ready. A clear idea of how much you are willing to back down on each issue will help you resolve the issues faster.

Sometimes, negotiations stall on certain issues. This could happen either when buyers do not anticipate this particular roadblock or when the importance of a particular issue is misjudged. This is a delicate situation. Sellers do not want to feel that their views are not respected, but at the same time, buyers do not want to spend too many days on a single issue. Try to amicably direct the negotiation to other issues on the list. If you have stalled on the price, you can agree to return to that discussion at a later point and start discussions on something else—say for instance, the buyer representations. Try to bring the discussion to something that pertains to you. This will make the seller feel less defensive and more receptive. This will also allow enough time for the buyer and the seller to think through mutually beneficial solutions.

Be prepared to walk away from the negotiation if the process is not going in the right direction. This can happen when the buyer and the seller disagree on vital issues. We do not advise negotiating and acquiring the business at any and every cost, unless it is really worth it. As mentioned before, buyers should be clear about the concessions to be made and try not to exceed those.

Negotiations are time bound. The negotiation is over when the buyer and the seller agree on the terms of sale and shake hands on the deal, or when one of them decides to walk away. Draft a letter of intent (see Chapter 13 for more details on this) that documents the terms of agreement. Have a lawyer review the letter of intent before giving it to the seller.

12.3   COMMON TRAPS AND TACTICS

Negotiation skills are a key component of entrepreneurial success. To some, negotiation is effortless and instinctive, but for most, it's a learned and acquired skill that takes time and practice to perfect. Some common traps in the process of negotiation include:

❖ Poor research that point to a price for the business without understanding the basis for the determination of the price. Ensure that the seller has researched his tax consequences as well. We have seen deals blow up when the seller finally asks his or her accountant how much tax liability he has. Ask the seller or his representative to make that call early in the process.

❖ Letting the first quoted price determine subsequent offers. This is an important difference. Treat the first quoted price as a kick start to negotiations, but not necessarily the starting price.

❖ Talking without listening. Listen carefully to the seller. Both verbal and non-verbal cues are important. The seller will definitely provide you some hints about negotiable and non-negotiable issues. Responding with sensitivity to the seller will help you secure the deal faster. Do not impose your views on the seller. Always remember that you are negotiating to make a purchase, and look for win-win situations.

❖ Letting emotions rule. Do not allow emotions or personalities to rule the process of negotiation. Focus on the issues.

❖ Lack of preparation. Do not assume that it is enough for you to turn up for the negotiation. Anticipate issues and prepare appropriate responses. You have to foresee the direction the negotiation is taking and try to bring it around to where you want it.

The best price is not going to be offered to you on a platter. You have to earn it the hard way. You may have to sit through several rounds of talks before you agree on terms. The better prepared and flexible you are, the more likely you will acquire the business.

Table 12.2 Some "don'ts"—common traps in negotiations
❖ Poor research
❖ Anchoring to the first quoted price
❖ Talking without listening
❖ Letting emotions rule
❖ Lack of preparation

Chapter 13

The Purchase Agreement

In this chapter, we will cover:
* What to include in a Letter of Intent
* What to include in a Purchase Agreement
* What Non-Compete Clauses are
* What Representations and Warranties are
* How to deal with contingencies

13.1   THE LETTER OF INTENT

Having got all the preliminary negotiation out of the way, you now need to formalize it. The Letter of Intent (LOI) is a document that summarizes the terms that the buyer and the seller have agreed upon during the negotiations. The LOI is a formal offer to the seller that indicates the willingness of the buyer to proceed with the acquisition of the business. The seller and the buyer sign the LOI. We have seen many buyers assume erroneously that the LOI is a sale deed. It is not a binding document, and does not indicate a formal contract between the buyer and the seller.

The contents of the LOI will depend on the negotiation with the seller and its outcome. Given that it is a not a legally binding document (with some exceptions noted below), the LOI is a useful but not an essential part of the transaction. You can actually proceed directly with a formal purchase agreement if you had a thorough discussion with the seller and have resolved all issues with clear terms of agreement.

There are three elements of the LOI that should be legally binding and that the LOI should make that clear: exclusivity, confidentiality, and non-binding disclaimer. The seller and his agents should not be out shopping the business during the negotiations (exclusivity). Both the seller and the buyer should protect the confidentiality of the information shared during the process. Everything else in the document is non-binding.

Figure 13.1 Items in a well-drafted LOI

The agreed price for the business

Structure of the sale: asset or stock

Terms of payment

List of assets that will be retained by the seller

Process for transfer of accounts receivables and other assets

List of liabilities to be assumed by buyer

Process to deal with transfer or payoff of liabilities

Terms of seller debt

Exclusivity

Non-compete terms

Schedule to complete discussions and formalize purchase agreement

Issues to be resolved

Proposed further investigations

Confidentiality clauses

Non-binding clause

13.2   WHAT TO INCLUDE IN A PURCHASE AGREE-MENT

The purchase agreement (PA) is a formal contract between the buyer and the seller. We recommend that a lawyer be involved in the preparation and review of the PA, as it is binding and open to legal challenges in case of any dispute.

Agreements of this nature tend to be swamped in legalese. Our advice is that you ensure that the language of the PA is clear and specific. Buyers have to make sure that they (in addition to the lawyers) understand the legal and contract jargon that is used in a PA. We have a very good reason for suggesting this—the buyer authenticates the information in this document, and he also agrees to uphold the clauses within when he signs it. As a buyer, you do not want to sign a document that you do not understand or cannot explain at a later date.

We also recommend that an accountant review the PA to ensure that there are no surprises regarding tax consequences at a later date.

Figure 13.2 Items in a well-drafted purchase agreement

Description of parties involved in transaction

Description of structure of deal

The final sale price and terms of payment

Description of the assets and liabilities of the company and disposition of each

Representations of the buyer and seller

Non-compete clauses

Future services

Contingencies

Closing documents

Process for resolution of disputes

Process to cover risk or loss

Clause to indicate that only what is in the purchase agreement is binding

Process for modification of the purchase agreement

The state whose law will govern the document

Severability clause that allows severance of the disputed part, leaving other parts of the agreement intact

Process for formal communications

Requisite signatures

13.3   NON-COMPETE CLAUSES

A seller could set up competing businesses with the proceeds of the sale, perhaps because this is an industry they are familiar with. You, as the buyer, would not want the seller to use your money to establish or join a competing business. A non-compete clause protects the buyer from such an eventuality. You have to make sure that you get the required signatures from all owners or sellers of the business.

The non-compete clause is not a lifelong commitment. It specifies a time frame, which is essentially the time that is needed to get the business up and running well under the new leadership. We advise buyers to make sure that this is a reasonable and comfortable time frame to settle into the business.

On the flip side, the non-compete clause can infringe upon the right of the seller to earn a livelihood. Buyers have to adequately compensate the seller and other co-owners for this potential loss of earnings. The compensation can be worked out with the seller such that both the buyer and the seller get optimal tax benefits. Buyers can work out a lower financial compensation for the non- compete clause. In such instances, buyers can increase the amount they pay for the assets or stock of the business. Buyers can also pay a higher compensation for the non- compete clause and reduce the price paid for the assets or stock.

13.4   REPRESENTATIONS AND WARRANTIES

Buyers receive information from the seller that helps them to reach the decision to acquire the business. Similarly, buyers provide information to the seller to convince him or her of their capability and commitment. These statements and assumptions form the representations and warranties section of the purchase agreement.

The target business provides details such as the list of patents it holds, trade secrets, trademarks, licenses, registered domain names, and copyrights. It also has to provide details of insurance policies, current liabilities, payroll tax, and employee benefit programs (healthcare, pension plans, etc.). It is important to document details of outstanding contracts that the business may have with vendors, suppliers, or customers.

This section of the document needs to explicitly mention tax implications from the acquisition. Finally, there has to be approval from the boards of participating companies as part of the purchase agreement.

Given the nature of the data being shared, there are serious legal consequences to statements that are later proved to be false. Scan the document to ensure you do not include any statement in the representation and warranty section unless you are absolutely sure of it. Faced with uncertainty over such statements, buyers generally qualify them with the preface: "To the best of the buyer's knowledge." The seller can similarly preface statements he or she is unsure of.

The representation and warranty clauses are usually worded such that they last beyond the closing of the deal, until the applicable statute of limitations runs out.

13.5   CONTINGENCIES

The contingency clause helps the buyer or the seller walk away from the deal with minimal losses if a particular condition is not met. The contingency clause is time bound, usually for a short period of time. This will help the buyer or the seller to move away from the deal quickly if it is necessary. Of course, the buyer or seller can also opt to extend the time period for the condition to be met.

Invoking a contingency clause to walk away from the deal will help the buyer get a refund of the deposit (if any). For example, you may introduce a contingency clause that the purchase will happen subject to your receiving satisfactory funding within a specified period. If you do not receive enough funding within this time frame, you can walk away from the deal with a refund of the deposit. Similarly, the seller may introduce a contingency clause that the sale will happen subject to being released from the terms of any lease within a specific time frame. The seller can invoke the clause to cancel the sale if this does not happen within the specified time frame. We recommend that buyers and sellers sign a mutual release document if the sale falls through, to prevent any legal consequences in future.

The information collected in the course of the due diligence exercise and research should guide you in framing the draft purchase agreement. By now, you, as the buyer, should be aware of the background, industry, operational model, organizational structure, assets, liabilities, and financial position of the target business. You should draw on this knowledge and information to come up with appropriate terms and conditions in the purchase agreement. However, note that the purchase agreement should address mutual benefits for both participating entities—the buyer and the target business.

Typically, there would be several follow-up meetings between both teams to discuss the purchase agreement, until they reach a position of mutual agreement on the terms and conditions laid down in the purchase agreement. It is very important to strike the right balance between comfort levels and yet be flexible to accommodate input from the target business. Please remember that this is not a battle for one-upmanship, but a step toward smooth and hassle-free closure of the deal.

It is also extremely important to understand that at the end of the day, you, as the buyer, own the documentation process for the purchase agreement. The buyer, rather than the team of professional advisors, should be in control of the process of drafting the purchase agreement. Once there is mutual agreement between the buyer and the seller on the purchase agreement, the buyer has to ensure that finances are secured, and the representations and information provided by the target business are re-validated.

This process of preparing the documentation is a step nearer to closing the deal. However, the deal is still open for termination, if both teams agree to the same in writing, or if the conditions as documented in the purchase agreement are not fulfilled.

Chapter 14

Making the Most of the Due Diligence Period

In this chapter, we will cover:
* What data to ask for
* What to do with the collected data

The buyer performs a due diligence exercise in the preliminary stages to ascertain the merits of the candidate for acquisition. Once he is convinced about the credentials of the target business, he drafts a letter of intent for the seller. You negotiate further with the seller and resolve all issues of importance to the transaction. You draw up a purchase agreement that details the discussions and terms of agreement between you and the seller. What happens next?

We recommend that you retrace your steps and engage in another round of due diligence, to determine the authenticity and accuracy of the information given to you before you finally close the deal.

The one approach we find very effective is also extremely simple. The buyer needs to create a checklist of questions that he should seek answers to. The checklist would typically be a mix of some generic questions, and certain other questions that are very specific to the situation. Some of the benefits of having such a checklist are:

- ❖ It will become a dynamic and alive document to capture the information that you receive in the course of your due diligence exercise
- ❖ Having a well-defined questionnaire and tracking responses to questions will ensure that you do not have vital facts falling through cracks
- ❖ It is very important to have a clear idea about the scope of the due diligence exercise, so that you can plan for timelines, effort required, and cost implications for this
- ❖ It will also help you decide the extent of expert guidance you may need for this activity

As you work on the checklist, make sure you prepare a comprehensive list of information and documentation you expect from the seller. More importantly, share this list with him, so that you set the right expectations. This also gives the seller time to start putting together the relevant information or documentation. Since the due diligence phase can actually be a long, drawn-out one, it helps to start quickly and involve key stakeholders early on.

Update the checklist when you receive information, and distribute it to the seller periodically (weekly updates would be appropriate) during the due diligence process. Everyone needs to be on the same page with respect to the status of the due diligence. Do not be surprised if one or more of the least important documents never materialize.

14.1   WHAT TO ASK FOR

A buyer's major concern is whether the representations made by the seller are accurate. You want to find out if what you intend to purchase is indeed what is promised. A buyer would like to ensure that the assets he receives are in the condition he expects, and the inventory he purchases measures up to the standards he set. This exercise aims to diffuse surprise liabilities that were not discussed during the negotiation. The detailed due diligence should cover three dimensions: business, financial, and legal.

We recommend that you involve your advisory team in the due diligence process. The support of experts will involve some expenditure, but can save you a lot more in retrospect.

From a business perspective, the due diligence should focus on operational aspects of the target business. The buyer may have to make several visits to the business to fully understand the dynamics involved. He will not only need to understand the evolution and growth of the business, but also its assets and liabilities.

You should customize the due diligence process based on the business you are buying.

Figure 14.1 Focus areas for operational due diligence

Evolution of the business

Operational issues

Products/services offered by the business

Market segment targeted by the business

Key relationships: customers, management, employees, suppliers

Nature of competition in the market where business operates

Details of facilities, assets, and liabilities

Corporate planning process

Internal control mechanisms

Sales and marketing strategies, and their effectiveness

Environmental issues

The financial aspect of the due diligence exercise requires validation of the financial information that you have been provided. This is where the buyer seeks assistance from his accountant or finance team. You may have the current value of the accounts receivables, but would need the seller or accountant to determine how much of the accounts receivable amount is actually recoverable. Checking on the age of accounts receivables may indicate that the collectable accounts receivables are actually lesser than those supplied.

Figure 14.2 Focus areas for financial due diligence

Detailed analysis of financial statements and the assumptions behind them

Review of accounting principles as relevant to the deal

Terms of loans

Details of leases

Assessing economic stability of business

Asset valuation

Risk evaluation and mitigation plans

Employee benefit schemes (health, pension)

Allocation of costs across various cost centers in the business

Identifying hidden costs

From a legal perspective, the due diligence exercise should focus on examining legal liabilities of the business and understanding the contractual obligations that the business currently has. It is very important to ensure that the seller does have the rights to sell the business. We recommend that your lawyer is involved through the entire process.

Pending litigation is critically important, both in a stock sale and in an asset sale. In a stock sale, you are acquiring those pending liabilities and will need indemnification from the seller. In an asset sale, the assets of the company may already be encumbered by the pending legal action, and free and clear title may be difficult to obtain. Pending or historical litigation may also be an indicator of how well the business is being managed.

Figure 14.3 Focus areas for legal due diligence

All key agreements of the business: customer, supplier, vendor agreements

Details of all liabilities, including loans, leases, and other financial arrangements

Details of intellectual property rights: patents, copyrights, trademarks

Corporate or business documents, including charter amendments, business bylaws, and minutes of key meetings

Employment terms for employees

Details of any ongoing legal proceedings pertinent to the business

Insurance-related documents

14.2 WHAT TO DO WITH THE COLLECTED DATA

Buyers will collect a lot of information during the due diligence process, and it often gets unwieldy. It is extremely important to analyze and interpret the information appropriately. An oversight could mean future expenses, wastage of time, and years of legal proceedings—surely not what you bargained for.

Have your advisors review each bit of information. Do not hesitate to ask them what each piece of information means, and how it can impact your purchase of the business. Ask for more details and clarifications from the seller if there is a need for more information. You can proceed with the deal if you are convinced that the information provided by the seller is accurate.

Ensure that you own the process. The due diligence process might uncover a lot of information that is not necessarily in your area of expertise. It is important that you drive the process, and understand the information and its interpretation. Your team of advisors can tell you what information to look for, what it means, and recommend a course of action. The final call still rests with you.

Table 14.1 Key considerations for the data collected through due diligence
❖ Have your team of advisors review the data
❖ Discuss with your team of advisors and understand the data
❖ Understand the implications on the business and on the purchase
❖ Take ownership of the final decision

Chapter 15
Choosing a Legal Form

In this chapter, we will cover:
* What General Partnerships are
* What Limited Liability Partnerships are
* What S Corporations are
* What C Corporations are
* Present a Summary Matrix

You have completed the due diligence process and have decided to acquire the business. You have to now decide what form your business will take. This is, to some extent, determined by the structure of the sale. If it is a stock sale, the acquisition will in all probability retain the original form of the business the buyer purchased. However, if it is an asset sale, the buyer needs to determine the business form. Choosing the appropriate form is important from a legal and financial perspective. We are not accountants or lawyers. We recommend that you discuss it with your lawyer and accountant.

15. 1   GENERAL PARTNERSHIPS

Partnerships are formed when two or more individuals join hands to run a for-profit company. A general partnership essentially shares ownership, assets, and liabilities equally among all partners. Partners share all profits and losses from the business; they share equal responsibility for the management and operations of the business; and are jointly or severally responsible for the liabilities of the business. No single partner can take ownership for the assets of the business, and each partner has unlimited liability for any obligations of the business. Each partner is taxed at the individual level on his or her share of the profits.

The general partnership is created through a documented agreement with details of the terms of agreement or partnership. The agreement normally terminates with death/disability/withdrawal of any partner from the partnership. However, most general partnership agreements address events like these, wherein the share of the departed/disabled/withdrawn partner is purchased by remaining partners. Disagreements for other ordinary matters pertaining to the administration of the organization are resolved through majority agreements. Disagreements of an extraordinary nature or amendments to partnership agreements require consensus. Unless otherwise indicated in the partnership agreement, new additions to the partnership are possible only through consensus of all partners in the general partnership. The general partnership is governed by the Uniform Partnership Act (UPA); however, the general partnership agreement supersedes the UPA in cases of any dispute.

15.2   LIMITED LIABILITY PARTNERSHIP

The limited liability partnership has partners with limited roles. Partners in such a partnership do not play an active role, as the general partners do. In fact, they cease to be a limited partner if they play an active role in the management of the business. Limited partners share in the profits and losses of the business, but have limited liability for any of its obligations, such as debts, contracts, mortgages, and so forth. The liability of the partner will not exceed the dollar value of the capital contributed by the partner. Each partner is taxed at the individual level on his or her share of the profits.

Each state has its own standards and regulations pertinent to the formation of a limited liability partnership. The agreements are complex and detailed, as the liability for the partners is limited. We recommend that you discuss each step with your lawyer and accountant before you proceed. Limited liability partnerships are not costly to set up, but you do not want your hard-earned cash going into a poorly drafted agreement that leaves you open to legal and financial liabilities.

15.3   S CORPORATIONS

An S corporation, in federal tax parlance, is a corporation that makes an election for taxation under subchapter S in Chapter 1 of the Internal Revenue Code, and satisfies the necessary criteria for consideration as an S corporation.

In order to make a valid election to be considered an S corporation, the business must fulfill the following criteria:

- ❖ Must be a domestic corporation, a partnership, or a single-member/multiple member limited liability company
- ❖ Must not have corporate shareholders
- ❖ Must not have non-resident shareholders
- ❖ Must not have more than thirty-five investors
- ❖ Must not be part of any affiliated group of corporations
- ❖ Must have only one class of stock

Generally, in an S corporation, instead of the organization paying corporate income taxes on profits, the shareholders pay income taxes on proportionate shares, also referred to as distributive shares, of the S corporation's profits. Shareholders are required to report income and pay appropriate taxes (if any), irrespective of whether shareholders receive actual cash distributions from the corporation. S corporations generally use shareholder agreements that provide for sufficient cash distribution to shareholders to enable them to pay taxes on their distributive shares. Quarterly estimated taxes are mandatory for shareholders in order to avoid tax penalties.

The organization must seek valid election to the S corporation status, typically within two and a half months from the start of the taxation year for which the election is being sought, or at any time during the year immediately before the relevant taxation year. However, based on instructions from Congress to demonstrate leniency toward late S elections, the IRS often accepts a late S election request. While S corporation is primarily a federal tax concept, there are some states, such as New York, that require a separate state-level S election for the corporation to be treated as an S corporation.

S corporations are often the preferred business form for acquisitions, since they are easy to form and allow owners to avoid double taxation.

15.4   C CORPORATIONS

A C corporation is a corporation that, for federal income tax purposes, is taxed under 26 U.S.C. § 11 and Subchapter C of Chapter 1 of the Internal Revenue Code.

A C corporation differs from an S corporation in several respects. Unlike an S corporation, a C corporation is taxed for its income. There is no limit on the number or nationality of shareholders in a C corporation.

The essential steps to the formation of a C corporation include:

❖ Choosing a business name that complies with the corporation rules of the state
❖ Appointment of initial directors
❖ Filing formal paperwork with filing fees—fees depend on the state of operation
❖ Laying down operating rules for the corporation
❖ Holding the first meeting of the board of directors
❖ Issuing stock certificates to initial shareholders
❖ Obtaining necessary licenses and permits

15.5   SUMMARY MATRIX

The following matrix sums up the relative merits and issues of the four options.

Comparison Factors	General Partnership (GP)	Limited Liability Partnership (LLP)	S Corporation (S Corp)	C Corporation (C Corp)
Business formation	State filing not needed, though some states allow filing at state agencies. A partnership agreement between two or more parties is mandatory.	Mandatory to file formation document with state agency. An operating agreement is required in most states.	Mandatory to file formation document with state agency. Most states mandate annual meetings and corporation laws. Must have valid election to S Corp status through IRS.	Mandatory to file formation document with state agency. Most states mandate annual meetings and corporation laws.
Size	Two or more individuals	Two or more members	Not exceeding 100 shareholders	Unlimited
Liability	General Partners are equally liable for debts or legal actions.	Members are not liable for debts of the company.	Shareholders are not liable for debts of the corporation. Some officers may be held responsible for fraud or misappropriation.	Shareholders are not liable for debts of the corporation. Some officers may be held responsible for fraud or misappropriation.

Opera-tional Procedures	Few legal requirements.	Most states have requirements like annual reports. Typically less than corporation.	Required to hold annual meetings, file paperwork, and publish reports. Board of directors and officers maintained.	Required to hold annual meetings, file paperwork, and publish reports. Board of directors and officers maintained.
Management	Typically, each partner has equal management authority.	Management responsibilities outlined in operating agreement.	Officers oversee day-to-day activities. Directors manage officers and oversee activities for the overall corporation. Directors are elected by shareholders.	Officers oversee day-to-day activities. Directors manage officers and oversee activities for the overall corporation. Directors are elected by shareholders.
Taxation	Once	Once	Once	Twice; both corporation and shareholders are taxed
Raising Capital	Contributed by participating partners	Some agreements allow interests to be sold	Selling stocks	Selling stocks

Dis-solution Complex-ity	Easy	Complex. Requires the filing of relevant documentation with state agency. Some states require tax clearance prior to dis-solution	More Complex. Requires the filing of relevant documenta-tion with state agency. Some states require tax clearance prior to dissolution	Most Com-plex. Requires the filing of relevant docu-mentation with state agency. Some states require tax clearance prior to dissolution

Chapter 16

Closing the Deal and Taking Control of Your Business

In this chapter, we will cover:
* ❋ How to get over the first day
* ❋ How to deal with employees
* ❋ How to deal with customers
* ❋ How to manage other key relationships

In preceding chapters, you have seen how to identify potential acquisition candidates, structure deals, raise finances for your purchase, perform thorough due diligence along business, financial, and legal dimensions, and finalize the purchase agreement—with professional guidance wherever needed. All that is left to do now is to close the deal and take control of your acquisition.

16.1   HOW TO GET OVER THE FIRST DAY

You have spent a fair amount of time understanding the business before you closed the deal. Needless to say, you will have a lot of ideas to improve the business further and will be eager to put all of these in place. We tell our clients to hold on to those ideas for a while. There will be plenty of time later to start making changes.

Spend the first day getting to know your employees and customers. You may have met some or all of them, and may even be on first-name basis. It still does not hurt to go over ground already covered or to bounce your new ideas off them. In the euphoria over having made the kill, buyers are often oblivious to the fact that employees will be apprehensive, both about the changes you may bring to the business and the potential impact on their continued employment. It is up to you to give them confidence that you have the best interests of the business and the employees at heart. Be prepared to spend the first day listening.

Buyers have spent considerable time studying and evaluating the target firm from afar; they now have the inside run. They need to spend the first day using this new vantage point to review the strengths and weaknesses. Check the list of changes that you wish to make and see if it still holds. If necessary, tweak the list of changes that you aim to implement.

Spend time with the customers, assuring them that the standards of the business will not change for the worse. It will not harm you to call the suppliers and let them know that you care for them.

Remember that change is often a gradual process that evolves over time and involves multiple stakeholders. While you may have thought through these changes during the due diligence period or the transition phase, key stakeholders like vendors, suppliers, employees, and customers might be taken by surprise. As far as possible, discuss potential changes with key stakeholders before implementation. You don't want to be the proverbial bull in the china shop. A common piece of advice often heard in this situation is: "Don't change anything for twelve months." Not always possible, but good advice nonetheless.

> Figure 16.1 Key considerations for the first day
> Meet all employees, as a group or individually
> Discuss the future direction of the business with employees
> Have a "cooling-off period" for the changes you wish to make to the business
> "Listen and learn" during the transition phase

16.2   HOW TO DEAL WITH EMPLOYEES

It is important that you address the concerns of the employees in a fair manner; this is one way you can retain the best employees. One option that many of our clients consider is to discuss their plans for the business in a town hall meeting with all employees. Possibly, this meeting will be the first time some of the employees interact with you. Try to give the employees a patient hearing and reply to issues raised by them.

Next, the new owner could plan an individual meeting with each employee. They spend this time gauging the strengths the employee brings to the business and his or her potential weaknesses. One positive approach would be to check if it is possible to address those weaknesses in a manner that will help the business grow. Sometimes, all that may be needed is a reorganization of the job profiles. For example, you may find that someone who is gregarious and fits the bill for sales is actually sitting behind the cash counter.

You may choose to seek expert advice for the interviewing process. Treat this as a process not only to judge how the employees qualify for their current roles and responsibilities, but also to understand their aspirations. It is also very important to keep the organizational culture in perspective during the decision-making process.

As the buyer soaks in the work culture at his new firm and makes decisions related to employees, he needs to ensure that he is taking into consideration the labor laws in force, because a labor lawsuit is the last thing he would want at this stage. We recommend that you seek professional assistance from a labor attorney in this regard. Remember, in an asset sale each employee is being terminated by the old company and "hired" into the new company. You may take this opportunity to "clean up" the employee roll and eliminate positions that may not be necessary in the new company. We see this issue mostly with relatives who are on the payroll (whether they work or not).

If employee commitment is important, so is employee compensation and management. Buyers need to take stock of the existing compensation strategy. Are employees compensated fairly? Do employees understand the basis for the compensation package? You might want to consider linking employee compensation at all levels to organizational performance. Employees will figure out that the contribution made toward organizational growth will be rewarded. And this should apply not only to the management cadre, but to all levels of employees. Allow the in-house team of human resource managers to bring you up to speed on their views and ideas.

Current management thought and our experience shows that it is advisable to actively involve employees in the change process. Ultimately, they are the ones who have to run with the idea on the ground. Try to understand the potential impact of the change process on each employee. Make sure you take time off to discuss the change with relevant employees. It might take some time to gain employee buy in, but it is well worth the wait compared to the energy and effort you may have to expend trying to implement an idea that no one buys into.

16.3   HOW TO DEAL WITH CUSTOMERS

New owners soon discover that they have to spend considerable time cultivating the existing customers of the business. The customer essentially will look at the quality of service and the personalized attention he receives. He will also be studying the changes closely to see if he is going to be inconvenienced in any way. You want to convince customers that you have their best interests at heart.

There are different ways of reaching out to customers. One way is to have personal one-on-one interactions with customers. But this will mean a lot of interactions if the business is large. The new owner can also consider group meetings or open houses to get to know each other better. He could also personally call the most valuable customers who bring in good business, set an appointment, and meet them. This would reassure them that the change of ownership will not affect their value to the business. Special offers to existing customers, such as discounts and value-added gifts, are some other ways to reach out and build bridges. We had a client who spent the first week on the phone, talking to all key customers personally. Each talk was followed by the delivery of a gift basket, showing his appreciation for their support of the business.

The more time you spend cultivating your customer base, the more likely you are to get good returns on your business.

16.4   OTHER KEY RELATIONSHIPS

Relationships with suppliers are an important component for the success of the business. It is very important to nurture these relationships and ensure that the acquisition does not create an air of uncertainty among these key business stakeholders.

Interact personally with key suppliers. It helps if the exiting owner introduces you to them during the transition process. Be open-minded and seek their advice on how to further strengthen these relationships. Talk to them about any concerns they have regarding the working relationship. Are there ways to improve the working relationship? You might want to schedule a round of one-on-one meetings with them, to let them know you care about them.

Sometimes, an in-depth analysis of these relationships may indicate that some of them may not be competitive or beneficial to the organization. One of our clients found out that a longstanding supplier was overcharging, and that he could get better terms elsewhere. The previous owner had apparently turned a blind eye because of the personal rapport they had. Our client tried to negotiate a better deal, and when that attempt failed he terminated the relationship with the supplier. Our client felt that the long-term gains were much higher than the short-term loss in this instance. The transition period is a good time to evaluate relationships and determine which ones should be terminated and which should be nurtured.

Make sure that you reach out to bankers, accountants, attorneys, and other professionals you retained through the acquisition. They walked through the deal with you and made it easier.

Managing relationships is not a one-time affair. Make sure you have scheduled enough time to interact with key stakeholders on a regular basis. Businesses thrive on relationships that are best managed through open-mindedness, free and fair communication, and sensitivity.

17.   CONCLUSION

We spent the last 16 chapters providing a framework with two purposes. First, we asked the questions you need to ask yourself to determine if buying a business is right for you. We fully expect that a significant proportion of you will decide buying a business is not right for you. You just are not comfortable that you can assemble a team of advisors, dig out opportunities, analyze the opportunities, acquire financing and close the deal. The risks associated with personal liability for the debts of the business are just too much to handle.

Second, we gave you an outline you can use to construct a plan specific to your situation. The major tasks required to find, evaluate and close a business purchase are detailed with a number of caveats regarding what can go wrong. We identified the advisors required to lower the risk and ensure that you get the right deal. You should understand that it really is hard work to buy a business. The financial rewards can be substantial if you are willing to do the work.

Of course, once you buy the business you still need to ensure that it is successful. In our experience, the first year after the acquisition will be a transition period. Historic profitability might not be attained due to additional debt, market changes or other fctors not evident during the acquisition process. Employees, customers and competitors recognize something changed and may behave differently sometimes, but not necessarily, for the better.

Remember, the first acquisition is the hardest.